C# Language
Pocket Reference

C# Language
Pocket Reference

Peter Drayton, Ben Albahari,
and Ted Neward

O'REILLY®

Beijing · Cambridge · Farnham · Köln · Paris · Sebastopol · Taipei · Tokyo

C# Language Pocket Reference

by Peter Drayton, Ben Albahari, and Ted Neward

Copyright © 2003 O'Reilly Media, Inc. All rights reserved.
Printed in the United States of America.

Published by O'Reilly Media, Inc., 1005 Gravenstein Highway North,
Sebastopol, CA 95472.

O'Reilly Media, Inc. books may be purchased for educational,
business, or sales promotional use. Online editions are also available
for most titles (*safari.oreilly.com*). For more information, contact our
corporate/institutional sales department: (800) 998-9938 or
corporate@oreilly.com.

Editors:	Brian Jepson and Nancy Kotary
Production Editor:	Mary Brady
Cover Designer:	Ellie Volckhausen
Interior Designer:	David Futato

Printing History:

November 2002:   First Edition.

0-596-00429-X
[C]

Contents

C# Language Pocket Reference

C# is a programming language from Microsoft that is designed specifically to target the .NET Framework. Microsoft's .NET Framework is a runtime environment and class library that dramatically simplifies the development of modern, component-based applications.

Microsoft has shown an unprecedented degree of openness in C# and the .NET Framework. The key specifications for the C# language and the .NET platform have been published, reviewed, and ratified by an international standards organization called the European Computer Manufacturers Association (ECMA). This standardization effort has led to a Shared Source release of the specification called the Shared Source CLI (*http://msdn.microsoft.com/net/sscli/*), as well as to Open Source implementations of .NET called DotGNU Portable .NET (*http://www.dotgnu.org*) and Mono (*http://www.go-mono.com*). All three implementations include support for C#.

This book is a quick-reference manual to the C# language as of version 1.0 of the .NET Framework. It lists a concise description of language syntax and provides a guide to other areas of the .NET Framework that are of interest to C# programmers.

The purpose of this quick reference is to aid readers who need to look up some basic detail of C# syntax or usage. It is not intended to be a tutorial or user guide, and at least a basic familiarity with C# is assumed. If you'd like more in-depth information or a more detailed reference, please see *Programming C#* by Jesse Liberty and *C# in a Nutshell* by Drayton, Albahari, and Neward (both O'Reilly, 2002).

Identifiers and Keywords

Identifiers are names programmers choose for their types, methods, variables, etc. An identifier must be a whole word that is essentially made up of Unicode characters starting with a letter or an underscore, and it may not clash with a keyword. As a special case, the @ prefix may be used to avoid a clash with a keyword, but is not considered part of the identifier. For instance, the following two identifiers are equivalent:

```
КоЯn
@КоЯn
```

C# identifiers are case-sensitive; however, for compatibility with other languages, you should not differentiate public or protected identifiers by case alone.

Here is a list of C# keywords:

abstract	as	base	bool	break
byte	case	catch	char	checked
class	const	continue	decimal	default
delegate	do	double	else	enum
event	explicit	extern	false	finally
fixed	float	for	foreach	goto
if	implicit	in	int	interface
internal	is	lock	long	namespace
new	null	object	operator	out
override	params	private	protected	public
readonly	ref	return	sbyte	sealed

short	sizeof	stackalloc	static	string
struct	switch	this	throw	true
try	typeof	uint	ulong	unchecked
unsafe	ushort	using	virtual	void
while				

Fundamental Elements

A C# program is best understood in terms of three basic elements:

Functions
> Perform an action by executing a series of statements. For example, you may have a function that returns the distance between two points or a function that calculates the average of an array of values. A function is a way of manipulating data.

Data
> Values that functions operate on. For example, you may have data holding the coordinates of a point or data holding an array of values. Data always has a particular type.

Types
> A set of data members and function members. The function members are used to manipulate the data members. The most common types are classes and structs, which provide a template for creating data. Data is always an instance of a type.

Value and Reference Types

All C# types fall into the following categories:

- Value types (struct, enum)
- Reference types (class, array, delegate, interface)

The fundamental difference between the two main categories is how they are handled in memory. The following sections explain the essential differences between value types and reference types.

Value Types

Value types directly contain data, such as the int type (which holds an integer) or the bool type (which holds a true or false value). The key characteristic of a value type is a copy made of the value that is assigned to another value. For example:

```
using System;
class Test {
  static void Main () {
    int x = 3;
    int y = x; // assign x to y, y is now a copy of x
    x++; // increment x to 4
    Console.WriteLine (y); // prints 3
  }
}
```

Reference Types

Reference types are a little more complex. A reference type defines two separate entities: an object and a reference to that object. This example follows the same pattern as our previous example, except that the variable y is updated here, while y remained unchanged earlier:

```
using System;
using System.Text;
class Test {
  static void Main () {
    StringBuilder x = new StringBuilder ("hello");
    StringBuilder y = x;
    x.Append (" there");
    Console.WriteLine (y); // prints "hello there"
  }
}
```

This is because the StringBuilder type is a reference type, while the int type is a value type. When we declared the StringBuilder variable, we were actually doing two different things, which can be separated into these two lines:

```
StringBuilder x;
x = new StringBuilder ("hello");
```

The first line creates a new variable that can hold a reference to a StringBuilder object. The second line assigns a new StringBuilder object to the variable. Let's look at the next line:

```
StringBuilder y = x;
```

When we assign x to y, we are saying "make y point to the same thing that x points to." A reference stores the address of an object. (An address is a memory location, stored as a 4-byte number.) We're actually still making a copy of x, but we're copying this 4-byte number as opposed to the StringBuilder object itself.

Let's look at this line:

```
x.Append (" there");
```

This line actually does two things. It first finds the memory location represented by x, and then it tells the StringBuilder object that lies at that memory location to append " there" to it. We could achieve exactly the same effect by appending " there" to y, because x and y refer to the same object:

```
y.Append (" there");
```

A reference may point to no object by assigning the reference to null. In this code sample, we assign null to x, but we can still access the same StringBuilder object we created via y:

```
using System;
using System.Text;
class Test {
  static void Main () {
    StringBuilder x;
    x = new StringBuilder ("hello");
```

```
      StringBuilder y = x;
      x = null;
      y.Append (" there");
      Console.WriteLine (y); // prints "hello there"
   }
}
```

Value and reference types side-by-side

A good way to understand the difference between value and reference types is to see them side-by-side. In C#, you can define your own reference types or your own value types. If you want to define a simple type such as a number, it makes sense to define a value type, in which efficiency and copy-by-value semantics are desirable. Otherwise, you should define a reference type. You can define a new value type by declaring a struct, and define a new reference type by defining a class.

To create a value-type or reference-type instance, the constructor for the type may be called using the new keyword. A value-type constructor simply initializes an object. A reference-type constructor creates a new object on the heap and then initializes the object:

```
// Reference-type declaration
class PointR {
  public int x, y;
}
// Value-type declaration
struct PointV {
  public int x, y;
}
class Test {
  static void Main() {
    PointR a; // reference type
    a = new PointR();

    PointV b; // value type
    b = new PointV();

    a.x = 7;
    b.x = 7;
  }
}
```

At the end of the method, the local variables a and b go out of scope, but the new instance of a PointR remains in memory until the garbage collector determines it is no longer referenced.

Assignment to a reference type copies an object reference, while assignment to a value type copies an object value:

```
    ...
    PointR c = a;
    PointV d = b;
    c.x = 9;
    d.x = 9;
    Console.WriteLine(a.x); // Prints 9
    Console.WriteLine(b.x); // Prints 7
  }
}
```

As shown in this example, an object on the heap can be pointed to by multiple variables, whereas an object on the stack or inline can only be accessed via the variable with which it was declared. *Inline* means that the variable is part of a larger object; i.e., it exists as a data member or an array member.

Boxing and unboxing value types

So that common operations can be performed on both reference and value types, each value type has a corresponding hidden reference type. This is created when it is assigned to an instance of System.Object or to an interface. This process is called *boxing*. A value type may be cast to the "object" class (the ultimate base class for all value types and reference types) or to an interface it implements.

In this example, we box and unbox an int value type to and from its corresponding reference type:

```
class Test {
  static void Main () {
    int x = 9;
    object o = x; // box the int
    int y = (int)o; // unbox the int
  }
}
```

When a value type is boxed, a new reference type is created to hold a copy of the value type. Unboxing copies the value from the reference type back into a value type. Unboxing requires an explicit cast, and a check is made to ensure that the value type to which you'd like to convert matches the type contained in the reference type. An InvalidCastException is thrown if the check fails. You never need to worry about what happens to boxed objects once you've finished with them: the garbage collector take cares of them for you.

Using collection classes is a good example of boxing and unboxing. In the following code, we use the Queue class with value types:

```
using System;
using System.Collections;
class Test {
  static void Main () {
    Queue q = new Queue ();
    q.Enqueue (1); // box an int
    q.Enqueue (2); // box an int
    Console.WriteLine ((int)q.Dequeue()); // unbox an int
    Console.WriteLine ((int)q.Dequeue()); // unbox an int
  }
}
```

Predefined Types

All of C#'s predefined types alias types found in the System namespace. For example, there is only a syntactic difference between these two statements:

```
int i = 5;
System.Int32 i = 5;
```

Integral Types

This table lists the integral types and their features:

C# type	System type	Size	Signed
sbyte	System.SByte	1 byte	Yes
short	System.Int16	2 bytes	Yes

C# type	System type	Size	Signed
int	System.Int32	4 bytes	Yes
long	System.Int64	8 bytes	Yes
byte	System.Byte	1 byte	No
ushort	System.UInt16	2 bytes	No
uint	System.UInt32	4 bytes	No
ulong	System.UInt64	8 bytes	No

For unsigned integers that are n bits wide, possible values range from 0 to 2. For signed integers that are n bits wide, their possible values range from -2^{n-1} to $2^{n-1}-1$. Integer literals can use either decimal or hexadecimal notation:

```
int x = 5;
ulong y = 0x1234AF; // prefix with 0x for hexadecimal
```

When an integral literal is valid for several possible integral types, the default type that is chosen goes in this order: int, uint, long, and ulong. The following suffixes may be used to specify the chosen type explicitly:

U

uint or ulong

L

long or ulong

UL

ulong

Integral conversions

An implicit conversion between integral types is permitted when the type to which you'd like to convert contains every possible value of the type to convert. Otherwise, an explicit conversion is required. For instance, you can implicitly convert an int to a long, but must explicitly convert an int to a short:

```
int x = 123456;
long y = x; // implicit, no information lost
short z = (short)x; // explicit, truncates x
```

Floating-Point Types

C# type	System type	Size
float	System.Single	4 bytes
double	System.Double	8 bytes

A float can hold values from approximately $\pm 1.5 \times 10^{-45}$ to approximately $\pm 3.4 \times 10^{38}$ with 7 significant figures.

A double can hold values from approximately $\pm 5.0 \times 10^{-324}$ to approximately $\pm 1.7 \times 10^{308}$ with 15–16 significant figures.

Floating-point types can hold the special values +0, –0, +∞, –∞, NaN (not a number). These represent the outcome of mathematical operations such as division by zero. float and double implement the specification of the IEEE 754 format types, supported by almost all processors, defined by the IEEE at *http://www.ieee.org*.

Floating-point literals can use decimal or exponential notation. A float literal requires the suffix f or F. A double literal may choose to add the suffix d or D.

```
float x = 9.81f;
double y = 7E-02; // 0.07
```

Floating-point conversions

An implicit conversion from a float to a double loses no information and is permitted, but not vice versa. An implicit conversion from an int, uint, and long to a float—and from a long to a double—is allowed for readability:

```
int strength = 2;
int offset = 3;
float x = 9.53f * strength - offset;
```

If this example uses larger values, precision may be lost. However, the possible range of values is not truncated, since both a float and a double's lowest and highest possible values exceed an int, uint, or long's lowest or highest value. All other conversions between integral and floating-point types must be explicit:

```
float x = 3.53f;
int offset = (int)x;
```

Decimal Type

The decimal type can hold values from $\pm 1.0 \times 10^{-28}$ to approximately $\pm 7.9 \times 10^{28}$ with 28–29 significant figures.

The decimal type holds 28 digits and the position of the decimal point on those digits. Unlike a floating-point value, it has more precision but a smaller range. It is typically useful in financial calculations, in which the combination of its high precision and the ability to store a base 10 number without rounding errors is very valuable. The number 0.1, for instance, is represented exactly with a decimal, but is represented as a recurring binary number with a floating-point type. There is no concept of +0, –0, +∞, –∞, and NaN for a decimal.

A decimal literal requires the suffix m or M.

```
decimal x = 80603.454327m; // holds exact value
```

Decimal conversions

An implicit conversion from all integral types to a decimal type is permitted because a decimal type can represent every possible integer value. A conversion from a decimal to floating type or vice versa requires an explicit conversion, since floating-point types have a bigger range than a decimal and a decimal has more precision than a floating-point type.

Char Type

C# type	System type	Size
char	System.Char	2 bytes

The char type represents a Unicode character. A char literal consists of either a character, Unicode format, or escape character enclosed in single quote marks:

```
'A' // simple character
'\u0041' // Unicode
'\x0041' // unsigned short hexadecimal
'\n' // escape sequence character
```

Table 1 lists the escape sequence characters.

Table 1. Escape sequence characters

Char	Meaning	Value
\'	Single quote	0x0027
\"	Double quote	0x0022
\\	Backslash	0x005C
\0	Null	0x0000
\a	Alert	0x0007
\b	Backspace	0x0008
\f	Form feed	0x000C
\n	New line	0x000A
\r	Carriage return	0x000D
\t	Horizontal tab	0x0009
\v	Vertical tab	0x000B

Char conversions

An implicit conversion from a char to most numeric types works—it's dependent upon whether the numeric type can accommodate an unsigned short. If it cannot, an explicit conversion is required.

Bool Type

C# type	System type	Size
bool	System.Boolean	1 byte/2 byte

The bool type is a logical value that can be assigned the literal true or false.

Although a boolean value requires only 1 bit (0 or 1), it occupies 1 byte of storage, since this is the minimum chunk with which addressing on most processor architectures can work. Each element in a boolean array uses two bytes of memory.

Bool conversions

No conversions can be made from booleans to numeric types or vice versa.

Object Type

C# type	System type	Size
object	System.Object	0-byte/8-byte overhead

The object class is the ultimate base type for both value types and reference types. Value types have no storage overhead from an object. Reference types, which are stored on the heap, intrinsically require an overhead. In the .NET runtime, a reference-type instance has an 8-byte overhead, which stores the object's type as well as its temporary information, such as its synchronization lock state or whether it has been fixed from movement by the garbage collector. Note that each reference to a reference-type instance uses 4 bytes of storage.

String Type

C# type	System type	Size
string	System.String	20-byte minimum

The C# string represents an immutable sequence of Unicode characters, and aliases the System.String class.

Although string is a class, its use is so ubiquitous in programming that it is given special privileges by both the C# compiler and the .NET runtime.

Unlike other classes, a new instance can be created using a string literal:

```
string a = "Heat";
```

Strings can also be created with verbatim string literals. Verbatim string literals start with @ and indicate that the string should be used verbatim, even if it spans multiple lines or includes escape characters (i.e., \). In this example, the pairs a1 and a2 represent the same string, and the pairs b1 and b2 represent the same string:

```
string a1 = "\\\\server\\fileshare\\helloworld.cs";
string a2 = @"\\server\fileshare\helloworld.cs";
Console.WriteLine(a1==a2); // Prints "True"

string b1 = "First Line\r\nSecond Line";
string b2 = @"First Line
Second Line";
Console.WriteLine(b1==b2); // Prints "True"
```

Arrays

Arrays allow a group of elements of a particular type to be stored in a contiguous block of memory. An array is specified by placing square brackets after the element type. For example:

```
int[] nums = new int[2];
nums[0] = 100;
nums[1] = 200;
char[] vowels = new char[] {'a','e','i','o','u'};
Console.WriteLine(vowels [1]); // Prints "e"
```

That last line prints "e" because array indexes start at 0. To support other languages, .NET can create arrays based on arbitrary start indexes, but all the libraries use zero-based indexing. Once an array is created, its length cannot be changed. However, the System.Collection classes provide dynamically sized arrays, as well as other data structures, such as associative (key/value) arrays.

Multidimensional Arrays

Multidimensional arrays come in two varieties: rectangular and jagged. Rectangular arrays represent an *n*-dimensional block, while jagged arrays are arrays of arrays. In this example we make use of the for loop, which is explained later in the "Statements" section. The for loops here simply iterate through each item in the arrays.

```
// rectangular
int [,,] matrixR = new int [3, 4, 5]; // creates 1 big
                                       // cube
// jagged
int [][][] matrixJ = new int [3][][];
for (int i = 0; i < 3; i++) {
    matrixJ[i] = new int [4][];
    for (int j = 0; j < 4; j++)
        matrixJ[i][j] = new int [5];
}
// assign an element
matrixR [1,1,1] = matrixJ [1][1][1] = 7;
```

Local Field Array Declarations

For convenience, local and field declarations may omit the array type when assigning a known value, since the type is specified in the declaration anyway:

```
int[,] array = {{1,2},{3,4}};
```

Array Length and Rank

Arrays know their own length. For multidimensional array methods, the array's GetLength method returns the number of elements for a given dimension, which is from 0 (the outermost) to the array's rank-1 (the innermost).

```
// single dimensional
for(int i = 0; i < vowels.Length; i++);
// multi-dimensional
for(int i = 0; i < matrixR.GetLength(2); i++);
```

Bounds Checking

All array indexing is bounds-checked by the runtime, with
IndexOutOfRangeException thrown for invalid indices. Like
Java, this prevents program faults and debugging difficulties
while enabling code to execute with security restrictions.

Array Conversions

Arrays of reference types may be converted to other arrays,
using the same logic you would apply to its element type.
This is called *array covariance*. All arrays implement System.
Array, which provides methods to get and set elements
generically regardless of the array type.

Variables and Parameters

A variable represents a typed storage location. A variable can
be a local variable, parameter, array element, instance field,
or static field.

All variables have an associated type, which essentially
defines the possible values the variable can have and the
operations that can be performed on that variable. C# is
strongly typed, which means the set of operations that can be
performed on a type are enforced at compile time rather than
at runtime. In addition, C# is type-safe, which ensures that a
variable can be operated on via the correct type only with the
help of runtime checking (except in unsafe blocks).

Definite Assignment

All variables in C# must be assigned a value before they are
used. A variable is either explicitly assigned a value or automatically assigned a default value. Automatic assignment

occurs for static fields, class instance fields, and array elements not explicitly assigned a value. For example:

```
using System;
class Test {
  int v;
  // Constructors that initalize an instance of a Test
  public Test() {} // v will be automatically assigned to
                   // 0
  public Test(int a) { // explicitly assign v a value
    v = a;
  }
  static void Main() {
    Test[] tests = new Test [2]; // declare array
    Console.WriteLine(tests[1]); // ok, elements assigned
                                 // to null
    Test t;
    Console.WriteLine(t); // error, t not assigned before
                          // use
  }
}
```

Default Values

The default value for all primitive (or atomic) types is zero:

Type	Default value
Numeric types	0
Bool type	False
Char type	'\0'
Enum types	0
Reference type	Null

The default value for each field in a complex (or composite) type is one of these aforementioned values.

Parameters

A method has a sequence of parameters. Parameters define the set of arguments that must be provided for that method.

In this example, the method Foo has a single parameter p of type int:

```
static void Foo(int p) {++p;}
static void Main() {
  Foo(8);
}
```

Passing arguments by value

By default, arguments in C# are passed by value. This is by far the most common case and means a copy of the value is created when passed to the method:

```
static void Foo(int p) {++p;}
static void Main() {
  int x = 8;
  Foo(x); // make a copy of the value-type x
  Console.WriteLine(x); // x will still be 8
}
```

Assigning p a new value does not change the contents of x, since p and x reside in different memory locations.

Ref modifier

To pass by reference, C# provides the parameter modifier ref, which allows p and x to refer to the same memory locations:

```
static void Foo(ref int p) {++p;}
static void Main () {
  int x = 8;
  Foo(ref x); // send reference of x to Foo
  Console.WriteLine(x); // x is now 9
}
```

Now assigning p a new value changes the contents of x. This is usually the reason we want to pass by reference, though occasionally it is more efficient when passing large structs. Notice how the ref modifier and the method definition are required in the method call. This makes it very clear what's going on, and clears ambiguity since parameter modifiers change the signature of a method.

The ref modifier is essential when implementing a swap method:

```
class Test {
  static void Swap (ref string a, ref string b) {
    string temp = a;
    a = b;
    b = temp;
  }
  static void Main () {
    string x = "Bush";
    string y = "Gore";
    Swap(ref x, ref y);
    System.Console.WriteLine("x is {0}, y is {1}", x, y);
  }
}
```
Outputs: x is Gore, y is Bush

The out modifier

C# is a language that insists variables be assigned before use. It also provides the out modifier, which is the natural complement of the ref modifier. While a ref modifier requires that a variable be assigned a value before being passed to a method, the out modifier requires that a variable be assigned a value before *returning* from a method:

```
using System;
class Test {
  static void Split(string name, out string firstNames,
                    out string lastName) {
    int i = name.LastIndexOf(' ');
    firstNames = name.Substring(0, i);
    lastName = name.Substring(i+1);
  }
  static void Main() {
    string a, b;
    Split("Nuno Bettencourt", out a, out b);
    Console.WriteLine("FirstName:{0}, LastName:{1}", a,
                      b);
  }
}
```

The params modifier

The params parameter modifier may be specified on the last parameter of a method so that the method accepts any number of parameters of a particular type. For example:

```
using System;
class Test {
  static int Add(params int[] iarr) {
    int sum = 0;
    foreach(int i in iarr)
      sum += i;
    return sum;
  }
  static void Main() {
    int i = Add(1, 2, 3, 4);
    Console.WriteLine(i); // 10
  }
}
```

Expressions and Operators

An expression is a sequence of operators and operands that specifies a computation. C# has unary operators, binary operators, and one ternary operator. Complex expressions can be built because an operand may itself be an expression, such as the operand (1 + 2) shown in the following example:

```
((1 + 2) / 3)
```

Operator Precedence

When an expression contains multiple operators, the precedence of the operators controls the order in which the individual operators are evaluated. When the operators are of the same precedence, their associativity determines the order. Binary operators (except for assignment operators) are left-associative; i.e., they are evaluated from left to right. The assignment operators, unary operators, and the conditional operator are right-associative; i.e., they are evaluated from right to left. For example:

```
1 + 2 + 3 * 4
```

is evaluated as:

```
((1 + 2) + (3 * 4))
```

because * has a higher precedence than +, and + is a binary operator that is left-associative. You can insert parentheses to change the default order of evaluation. C# overloads operators, which means the same operator can have different meanings for different types.

Table 2 lists C#'s operators in order of precedence. Operators in the same box have the same precedence, and operators in italic may be overloaded for custom types.

Table 2. Operator precedence table

Category	Operators	Examples
Primary	Grouping:	`(x)`
	Member access:	`x.y`
	Struct pointer member access:	`->`
	Method call:	`f(x)`
	Indexing:	`a[x]`
	Post increment:	`x++`
	Post decrement:	`x--`
	Constructor call:	`new`
	Array stack allocation:	`stackalloc`
	Type retrieval:	`typeof`
	Struct size retrieval:	`sizeof`
	Arithmetic check on:	`checked`
	Arithmetic check off:	`unchecked`
Unary	*Positive value of (passive):*	`+`
	Negative value of:	`-`
	Not:	`!`
	Bitwise complement:	`~`
	Preincrement:	`++x`
	Predecrement:	`--x`
	Type cast:	`(T)x`
	Value at address:	`*`
	Address of value:	`&`
Multiplicative	*Multiply:*	`*`
	Divide:	`/`
	Division remainder:	`%`

Table 2. Operator precedence table (continued)

Category	Operators	Examples
Additive	*Add:* *Subtract:*	+ -
Shift	*Shift bits left:* *Shift bits right:*	<< >>
Relational	*Less than:* *Greater than:* *Less than or equal to:* *Greater than or equal to:* *Type equality/compatibility:* *Conditional type conversion:*	< > <= >= is as
Equality	*Equals:* *Not equals:*	== !=
Logical bitwise	And: Exclusive or: Or:	& ^ |

Logical Boolean	And:
	Or:
	Ternary conditional: ?:
	
	is equivalent to:
		&&
		||
		e.g., int x = a > b ? 2 : 7;
		
		int x; if (a > b) x = 2; else x = 7;

Assignment	Assign/modify:	= *= /= %= += -= <<= >>= &= ^= |=

Arithmetic Overflow Check Operators

The checked operator tells the runtime to generate an OverflowException if an integral expression exceeds the arithmetic limits of that type. The checked operator affects expressions with the ++, --, (unary)-, +, -, *, /, and explicit conversion operators between integral types. For example:

```
int a = 1000000;
int b = 1000000;

// Check an expression
int c = checked(a*b);
```

```
// Check every expression in a statement-block
checked {
    ...
    c = a * b;
    ...
}
```

The checked operator applies only to runtime expressions, since constant expressions are checked during compilation (though this can be turned off with the /checked [+|-] command-line switch). The unchecked operator disables arithmetic checking at compile time and is seldom useful, but does make expressions such as the following compile:

```
const int signedBit = unchecked((int)0x80000000);
```

Statements

Execution in a C# program is specified by a series of statements that execute sequentially in the textual order in which they appear. All statements in a procedural-based language such as C# are executed for their effect. For instance, a statement may assign an expression to a variable, repeatedly execute a list of statements, or jump to another statement.

So that multiple statements can be grouped together, zero or more statements may be enclosed in braces to form a statement block.

Expression Statements

An expression statement evaluates an expression, either assigning its result to a variable or generating side effects (i.e., method invocation, new, ++, --). An expression statement ends in a semicolon. For example:

```
int x = 5 + 6; // assign result
x++; // side effect
int y = Math.Min(x, 20); // side effect and assign result
Math.Min(x, y); // discards result, but ok, there is a
                // side effect
x == y; // error, has no side effect, and does not assign
        // result
```

Declaration Statements

A declaration statement declares a new variable, optionally assigning the result of an expression to that variable. A declaration statement ends in a semicolon:

```
int x = 100; // variable declaration
const int y = 110; // constant declaration
```

The scope of a local or constant variable extends to the end of the current block. You cannot declare another local variable with the same name in the current block or in any nested blocks. For example:

```
bool a = true;
while(a) {
  int x = 5;
  if (x==5) {
    int y = 7;
    int x = 2; // error, x already defined
  }
  Console.WriteLine(y); // error, y is out of scope
}
```

A constant declaration is like a variable declaration, except that the variable cannot be changed after it has been declared:

```
const double speedOfLight = 2.99792458E08;
speedOfLight+=10; // error
```

Selection Statements

C# has many ways to control the flow of program execution conditionally. This section covers the simplest two constructs: the if-else statement and the switch statement. In addition, C# also provides the operator and loop statements that conditionally execute based on a Boolean expression. Finally, C# provides object-oriented ways of conditionally controlling the flow of execution, namely virtual method invocations and delegate invocations.

The if-else statement

An if-else statement executes code depending on whether a Boolean expression is true. Unlike in C, only a Boolean expression is permitted. In this example, the Compare method returns 1 if a is greater than b, −1 if a is less than b, and 0 if a is equal to b.

```
int Compare(int a, int b) {
    if (a>b)
        return 1;
    else if (a<b)
        return -1;
    return 0;
}
```

It is very common to use the ||, &&, and ! operators to test for AND, OR, and NOT conditions. In this example, our GetUmbrellaNeeded method returns an umbrella if it's rainy or sunny (to protect us from the rain or the sun), as long as it's not also windy (since umbrellas are useless in the wind):

```
Umbrella GetUmbrella (bool rainy, bool sunny, bool windy)
{
    if ((rainy || sunny) && ! windy)
        return umbrella;
    return null;
}
```

The switch statement

switch statements let you branch program execution based on a selection of possible values a variable may have. switch statements may result in cleaner code than multiple if statements, since switch statements require that an expression be evaluated only once. For instance:

```
void Award(int x) {
  switch(x) {
    case 1:
      Console.WriteLine("Winner!");
      break;
    case 2:
      Console.WriteLine("Runner-up");
      break;
```

```
      case 3:
      case 4:
        Console.WriteLine("Highly commended");
        break;
      default:
        Console.WriteLine("Don't quit your day job!");
        break;
    }
  }
```

The switch statement can only evaluate a predefined type (including the string type) or enum, though user-defined types may provide an implicit conversion to these types.

The end of each case statement must be unreachable. This typically means each case statement ends with a jump statement. These are the options:

- Use the break statement to jump to the end of the switch statement. (This is by far the most common option.)

- Use the goto case <constant expression> or goto default statements to jump to either another case statement or to the default case statement.

- Use any other jump statement—namely, the return, throw, continue, or goto labels.

Unlike in Java and C++, the end of a case statement must explicitly state where to go next. There is no error-prone "default fall through" behavior; not specifying a break results in the next case statement being executed:

```
    void Greet(string title) {
      switch (title) {
        case null:
          Console.WriteLine("And you are?");
          goto default;
        case "King":
          Console.WriteLine("Greetings your highness");
          // error, should specify break, otherwise...
        default :
          Console.WriteLine("How's it hanging?");
          break;
      }
    }
```

Loop Statements

C# enables a sequence of statements to execute repeatedly with the while, do while, for, and foreach statements.

while loops

while loops repeatedly execute a statement block when a Boolean expression is true. The expression is tested before the statement block is executed. For example:

```
int i = 0;
while (i<3) {
  Console.WriteLine (i);
  i++;
}

Output:
0
1
2
```

do-while loops

do-while loops differ from while loops only in functionality in that they allow the expression to be tested after the statement block has executed. In this example, a do-while loop prints 8—a while loop would not print anything. For example:

```
int i = 8;
do {
  Console.WriteLine (i);
  i++;
} while (i<5);

Output:
8
```

for loops

for loops can be more convenient than while loops when you need to maintain an iterator value. As in Java and C, for loops contain three parts. The first part is a statement executed before the loop begins, and by convention it is used to initialize an iterator variable; the second part is a Boolean expression that, while true, executes the statement block; and the third part is a statement executed after each iteration of the statement block, in which convention is used to iterate the iterator variable. For example:

```
for (int i=0; i<10; i++)
  Console.WriteLine(i);
```

Any of the three parts of the for statement may be omitted. One can implement an infinite loop such as the following (though while (true) may be used instead):

```
for (;;)
  Console.WriteLine("Hell ain't so bad");
```

foreach loops

It is very common for for loops to iterate over a series of elements, so C#, like Visual Basic, has a foreach statement.

For instance, instead of doing the following:

```
for (int i=0; i<dynamite.Length; i++)
  Console.WriteLine(dynamite [i]);
```

You can perform this action:

```
foreach (Stick stick in dynamite)
  Console.WriteLine(stick);
```

The foreach statement works on any collection (including arrays). Although not strictly necessary, all collections leverage this functionality by supporting IEnumerable and IEnumerator (see the "Enumerating a Collection" topic in the .NET Framework SDK Documentation). Here is an equivalent way to iterate over our collection:

```
IEnumerator ie = dynamite.GetEnumerator();
while (ie.MoveNext()) {
  Stick stick = (Stick)ie.Current;
  Console.WriteLine(stick);
}
```

Jump Statements

The C# jump statements are break, continue, goto, return, and throw. All jump statements obey sensible restrictions imposed by try statements (see the later section "Try Statements and Exceptions"). First, a jump out of a try block always executes the try's finally block before reaching the target of the jump. Second, a jump cannot be made from the inside to the outside of a finally block.

The break statement

The break statement transfers execution from the enclosing while loop, for loop, or switch statement block to the next statement block.

```
int x = 0;
while (true) {
  x++;
  if (x>5)
    break; // break from the loop
}
```

The continue statement

The continue statement forgoes the remaining statements in the loop and makes an early start on the next iteration.

```
int x = 0;
int y = 0;
while (y<100) {
  x++;
  if ((x%7)==0)
    continue; // continue with next iteration
  y++;
}
```

The goto statement

The goto statement transfers execution to another label within the statement block. A label statement is just a placeholder in a method:

```
int x = 4;
start:
```

```
x++;
if (x==5)
  goto start;
```

You can use goto in a case statement to transfer execution to another case label in a switch block (as explained earlier in the "The switch statement" section).

The return statement

The return statement exits the method and must return an expression of the method's return type if the method is non-void.

```
int CalcX(int a) {
  int x = a * 100;
  return x; // return to the calling method with value
}
```

The throw statement

The throw statement throws an exception to indicate an abnormal condition has occurred (see the later section "Try Statements and Exceptions").

```
if (w==null)
  throw new ArgumentException("w can't be null");
```

The lock statement

The lock statement is actually a syntactic shortcut for calling the Enter and Exit methods of the System.Threading.Monitor class.

The using statement

Many classes encapsulate nonmemory resources, such as file handles, graphics handles, or database connections. These classes implement System.IDisposable, which defines a single parameterless method named Dispose called to clean up these resources. The using statement provides an elegant syntax for declaring and then calling the Dispose method of variables that implement IDisposable. For example:

```
using (FileStream fs =
    new FileStream (fileName, FileMode.Open))
```

```
    {
    ...
    }
```

This is precisely equivalent to:

```
FileStream fs = new FileStream (fileName, FileMode.Open);
try {
  ...
}
finally {
  if (fs != null)
    ((IDispoable)fs).Dispose();
}
```

Namespaces

These are defined in files, organized by namespaces, compiled into a module, then grouped into an assembly. These organizational units are cross-cutting. For example, typically a group of namespaces belong to one assembly, but a single namespace may in fact be spread over multiple assemblies.

Files

File organization is almost of no significance to the C# compiler—a whole project could be merged into one *.cs* file and it would still compile (preprocessor statements are the only exception to this). However, it's generally tidy to have one type in one file, with the filename matching the name of the class and the file's directory matching the name of the class's namespace.

Using Namespaces

A namespace lets you group related types into a hierarchical categorization. Generally, the first name is the name of your organization; it gets more specific from there:

```
namespace MyCompany.MyProduct.Drawing {
  class Point {int x, y, z;}
  delegate void PointInvoker(Point p);
}
```

Nesting namespaces

You may also nest namespaces instead of using dots. This example is semantically identical to the previous example:

```
namespace MyCompany {
  namespace MyProduct {
    namespace Drawing {
      class Point {int x, y, z;}
      delegate void PointInvoker(Point p);
    }
  }
}
```

Using a type with its fully qualified name

To use the Point from another namespace, you may refer to it with its fully qualified name. The namespace that a type is within actually becomes part of the type name:

```
namespace TestProject {
  class Test {
    static void Main() {
      MyCompany.MyProduct.Drawing.Point x;
    }
  }
}
```

The using keyword

The using keyword is a convenient way to avoid using the fully qualified name of types in other namespaces. This example is semantically identical to our previous example:

```
namespace TestProject {
  using MyCompany.MyProduct.Drawing;
  class Test {
    static void Main() {
      Point x;
    }
  }
}
```

Aliasing types and namespaces

Type names must be unique within a namespace. To avoid naming conflicts without having to use fully qualified names,

C# allows you to specify an alias for a type or namespace. Here is an example:

```
using sys = System;        // Namespace alias
using txt = System.String; // Type alias
class Test {
  static void Main() {
    txt s = "Hello, World!";
    sys.Console.WriteLine(s); // Hello, World!
    sys.Console.WriteLine(s.GetType()); // System.String
  }
}
```

Global namespace

The global namespace is the outermost level in which all namespaces and types are implicitly declared. When a type is not explicitly declared within a namespace, it may be used without qualification from any other namespace, since it is a member of the global namespace. However, apart from the smallest programs, it is always good practice to organize types within logical namespaces.

In this example, the class Example is declared in the global namespace, so it can be used without qualification from the Noo namespace.

```
class Test {
  public static void Foo () {
    System.Console.WriteLine ("hello!");
  }
}
namespace Noo {
  class Test2 {
    static void Main() {
      Test.Foo();
    }
  }
}
```

Classes

In C#, a program is built by defining new types, each with a set of data members and function members. Custom types should form higher-level building blocks that are easy to use and that closely model your problem space.

In this example, we simulate an astronaut jumping on different planets, using three classes—Planet, Astronaut, and Test—to test our simulation.

First, let's define the Planet class. By convention, we define the data members of the class at the top of the class declaration. There are two data members here, the name and gravity fields, which store the name and gravity of a planet. We then define a constructor for the planet. *Constructors* are function members that allow you to initialize an instance of your class. We initialize the data members with values fed to the parameters of the constructor. Finally, we define two more function members, which are properties that allow us to get the "Name" and "Gravity" of a planet. The Planet class looks like this:

```
using System;

class Planet {
  string name; // field
  double gravity; // field
  // constructor
  public Planet (string n, double g) {
    name = n;
    gravity = g;
  }
  // property
  public string Name {
    get {return name;}
  }
  // property
  public double Gravity {
    get {return gravity;}
  }
}
```

Next, we define the Astronaut class. As with the Planet class, we first define our data members. Here an astronaut has two fields: the astronaut's fitness and the current planet the astronaut is on. We then provide a constructor, which initializes the fitness of an astronaut. Next, we define a CurrentPlanet property that allows us to get or set the planet an astronaut is on. Finally, we define a jump method that outputs how far the astronaut jumps, based on the fitness of the astronaut and the planet he is on.

```
using System;

class Astronaut {
  double fitness; // field
  Planet currentPlanet; // field

  // constructor
  public Astronaut (double f) {
    fitness = f;
  }
  // property
  public Planet CurrentPlanet {
    get {
      return currentPlanet;
    }
    set {
      currentPlanet = value;
    }
  }
  // method
  public void Jump () {
    if (currentPlanet == null)
      Console.WriteLine ("Bye Bye!");
    else {
      double distance = fitness/currentPlanet.Gravity;
      Console.WriteLine ("Jumped {0} metres on {1}",
                         distance,
                         currentPlanet.Name);
    }
  }
}
```

Last, we define the Test class, which uses the Planet and Astronaut classes. Here we create two planets, earth and moon, and one astronaut, forestGump. Then we see how far forestGump jumps on each of these planets:

```
class Test {
  static void Main () {
    // create a new instance of a planet
```

```
      Planet earth = new Planet ("earth", 9.8);
      // create another new instance of a planet
      Planet moon = new Planet ("moon", 1.6);
      // create a new instance of an astronaut
      Astronaut forestGump = new Astronaut (20);
      forestGump.CurrentPlanet = earth;
      forestGump.Jump();
      forestGump.CurrentPlanet = moon;
      forestGump.Jump();
   }
}
```
Output:
```
Jumped 2.04081632653061 metres on earth
Jumped 12.5 metres on moon
```

If you save these to *Planet.cs*, *Astronaut.cs*, and *Test.cs*, you can compile them into *Test.exe* with this:

```
csc Test.cs Planet.cs Astronaut.cs
```

If a class is designed well, it becomes a new higher-level building block that is easy for someone else to use. The user of a class seldom cares about the data members or implementation details of another class...merely its specification. To use a Planet or an Astronaut, all you need to know is how to use their public function members.

In the following section, we look at each kind of type members a class can have, namely fields, constants, properties, indexers, methods, operators, constructors, destructors, and nested types.

The this Keyword

The this keyword denotes a variable that references a class or struct instance and is only accessible from within non-static function members of the class or struct. The this keyword is also used by a constructor to call an overloaded constructor (explained later) or declare or access indexers (also explained later). A common use of the this variable is to distinguish a field name from a parameter name:

```
using System;
class Dude {
  string name;
```

```
public Dude (string name) {
  this.name = name;
}
public void Introduce(Dude a) {
  if (a!=this)
    Console.WriteLine("Hello, I'm "+name);
}
}
```

Fields

Fields hold data for a class or struct:

```
class MyClass {
  int x;
  float y = 1, z = 2;
  static readonly int MaxSize = 10;
  ...
}
```

Nonstatic fields

Nonstatic fields are also referred to as instance variables or instance data members. Static variables are also referred to as static variables or static data members.

The readonly modifier

As the name suggests, the readonly modifier prevents a field from being modified after it has been assigned. Such a field is termed a *read-only field*. A read-only field is always evaluated at runtime, not at compile time. It must be assigned in its declaration or within the type's constructor for it to compile (see more on constructors later in this book). On the other hand, non-read-only fields merely generate a warning when left unassigned.

Constants

A constant is a field that is evaluated at compile time and is implicitly static. The logical consequence of this is that a constant may not defer evaluation to a method or constructor, and it may only be one of a few built-in types. These types are sbyte, byte, short, ushort, int, uint, long, ulong, float, double, decimal, bool, char, string, and enum. For example:

```
public const double PI = 3.14159265358979323846;
```

The benefit of a constant is that it is evaluated at compile time, permitting additional optimization by the compiler. For instance:

```
public static double Circumference(double radius) {
  return 2 * Math.PI * radius;
}
```

evaluates to:

```
public static double Circumference(double radius) {
  return 6.2831853071795862 * radius;
}
```

A read-only field would not make this optimization, but it is more versionable. For instance, suppose there is a mistake in the calculation of *pi*. Microsoft releases a patch to their library that contains the Math class, which is deployed to each client computer. If your software that uses the Circumference method is already deployed on a client machine, then the mistake is not fixed until you recompile your application with the latest version of the Math class. With a read-only field, however, this mistake is automatically fixed. Generally, this scenario occurs when a field value changes because of an upgrade (such as MaxThreads changing from 500 to 1,000), not as a result of a mistake.

Properties

Properties can be characterized as object-oriented fields. Properties promote encapsulation by allowing a class or struct to control access to its data and by hiding the internal representation of the data. For instance:

```
public class Well {
  decimal dollars; // private field
  public int Cents {
    get { return(int)(dollars * 100); }
```

```
  set {
    // value is an implicit variable in a set
    if (value>=0) // typical validation code
        dollars = (decimal)value/100;
  }
 }
}
class Test {
   static void Main() {
      Well w = new Well();
      w.Cents = 25; // set
      int x = w.Cents; // get
      w.Cents += 10; // get and set(throw a dime in the
                     // well)
   }
}
```

The get accessor returns a value of the property's type. The set accessor has an implicit parameter named value that is of the property's type. A property can be read-only if it specifies only a get method, and write-only if it specifies only a write method (though rarely desirable).

Indexers

Indexers provide a natural way of indexing elements in a class or struct that encapsulate a collection, via an array's [ ] syntax. Indexers are similar to properties, but they are accessed via an index, as opposed to a property name. The index can be any number of parameters. In the following example, the ScoreList class maintains the list of scores given by five judges. The indexer uses a single int index to get or set a particular judge's score.

```
public class ScoreList {
  int[] scores = new int [5];
  // indexer
  public int this[int index] {
    get {
      return scores[index]; }
    set {
      if(value >= 0 && value <= 10)
        scores[index] = value;
    }
```

```
    }
    // property (read-only)
    public int Average {
      get {
        int sum = 0;
        foreach(int score in scores)
          sum += score;
        return sum / scores.Length;
      }
    }
  }
  class Test {
    static void Main() {
      ScoreList sl = new ScoreList();
      sl[0] = 9;
      sl[1] = 8;
      sl[2] = 7;
      sl[3] = sl[4] = sl[1];
      System.Console.WriteLine(sl.Average);
    }
  }
```

A type may declare multiple indexers that take different parameters (or multiple parameters for multidimensional indexers). Our example could be extended to return the score by a judge's name, as opposed to a numeric index.

Indexers are compiled to get_Item (...)/set_Item (...) methods, which is the representation in MSIL.

```
public int get_Item (int index) {...}
public void set_Item (int index, int value) {...}
```

Methods

All C# code executes in a method or in a special form of a method. Constructors, destructors, and operators are special types of methods, and properties and indexers are internally implemented with get and set methods.

Signatures

A method's signature is characterized by the type and modifier of each parameter in its parameter list. The parameter modifiers ref and out allow arguments to be passed by reference, rather than by value. These characteristics are referred to as a *method signature* because they uniquely distinguish one method from another.

Overloading methods

A type may overload methods (have multiple methods with the same name), as long as the signatures are different.* For example, the following methods can all coexist in the same type:

```
void Foo(int x);
void Foo(double x);
void Foo(int x, float y);
void Foo(float x, int y);
void Foo(ref int x);
```

However, the following pairs of methods cannot coexist in the same type, since the return type and params modifier do not qualify as part of a method's signature.

```
void Foo(int x);
float Foo(int x); // compile error
void Goo (int[] x);
void Goo (params int[] x); // compile error
```

Instance Constructors

Constructors allow initialization code to perform for a class or struct. A class constructor first creates a new instance of that class on the heap and then performs initialization, while a struct constructor merely performs initialization.

Unlike ordinary methods, a constructor has the same name as the class or struct and has no return type:

```
class MyClass {
  public MyClass() {
    // initialization code
  }
}
```

* An exception to this rule is that two otherwise identical signatures cannot coexist if one parameter has the ref modifier and the other parameter has the out modifier.

A class or struct may overload constructors and may call one of its overloaded constructors before executing its method body using the this keyword:

```
using System;
class MyClass {
  public int x;
  public MyClass() : this(5) {}
  public MyClass(int v) {
    x = v;
  }
  static void Main() {
    MyClass m1 = new MyClass();
    MyClass m2 = new MyClass(10);
    Console.WriteLine(m1.x); // 5
    Console.WriteLine(m2.x); // 10
  }
}
```

If a class does not define any constructors, an implicit parameter-free constructor is created. A struct cannot define a parameter-free constructor, since a constructor that initializes each field with a default value (effectively zero) is always implicitly defined.

Field initialization order

Another useful way to perform initialization is to assign fields an initial value in their declaration:

```
class MyClass {
  int x = 5;
}
```

Field assignments are performed before the constructor is executed and are initialized in the textual order in which they appear.

Constructor access modifiers

A class or struct may choose any access modifier for a constructor. It is occasionally useful to specify a private constructor to prevent a class from being constructed. This is appropriate for utility classes made up entirely of static members, such as the System.Math class.

Static Constructors

A *static constructor* allows initialization code to execute before the first instance of a class or struct is created or before any static member of the class or struct is accessed. A class or struct can define only one static constructor, and it must be parameter-free and have the same name as the class or struct:

```
class Test {
    static Test() {
        Console.WriteLine("Test Initialized");
    }
}
```

Static field initialization order

Each static field assignment is made before any of the static constructors are called, and they are initialized in the textual order in which they appear, which is consistent with instance fields.

```
class Test {
  public static int x = 5;
  public static void Foo() {}
  static Test() {
    Console.WriteLine("Test Initialized");
  }
}
```

Accessing either Test.x or Test.Foo assigns 5 to x and then prints Test Initialized.

Nondeterminism of static constructors

Static constructors cannot be called explicitly, and the runtime may invoke them well before they are first used. Programs should not make any assumptions about the timing of a static constructor's invocation. In this example, Test Initialized may be printed after Test2 Initialized:

```
class Test2 {
  public static void Foo() {}
  static Test2 () {
```

```
      Console.WriteLine("Test2 Initialized");
    }
}
...
Test.Foo();
Test2.Foo();
```

Destructors and Finalizers

Destructors are class-only methods that are used to clean up nonmemory resources just before the garbage collector reclaims the memory for an object:

```
class Test {
  ~Test() {
    // destructor code here
  }
}
```

Just as a constructor is called when an object is created, a destructor is called when an object is destroyed. C# destructors are very different from C++ destructors, primarily because of the presence of the garbage collector. First, memory is automatically reclaimed with a garbage collector, so a destructor in C# is used solely for nonmemory resources. Second, destructor calls are nondeterministic. The garbage collector calls an object's destructor when it determines that it is no longer referenced; however, it may determine this after an undefined period of time has passed since the last reference to the object disappeared.

Nested Types

A nested type is declared within the scope of another type. Nesting a type has three benefits:

- A nested type can access all the members of its enclosing type, regardless of a member's access modifier.
- A nested type can be hidden from other types with type-member access modifiers.

- Accessing a nested type from outside of its enclosing type requires specifying the type name. This is the same principle used for static members.

For example:

```
using System;
class A {
  int x = 3; // private member
  protected internal class Nested {// choose any access-
                                   // level
    public void Foo () {
      A a = new A ();
      Console.WriteLine (a.x); // can access A's private
                              // members
    }
  }
}
class B {
  static void Main () {
    A.Nested n = new A.Nested (); // Nested is scoped to A
    n.Foo ();
  }
}
// an example of using "new" on a type declaration
    class C : A {
    new public class Nested {} // hide inherited type
                              // member
}
```

Access Modifiers

To promote encapsulation, a type or type member may hide itself from other types or other assemblies by adding one of the following five access modifiers to the declaration:

public

The type or type member is fully accessible. This is the implicit accessibility for enum members (see the later section "Enums") and interface members (see the later section "Interfaces").

internal

    The type or type member in assembly *A* is accessible only from within *A*. This is the default accessibility for non-nested types, and so it may be omitted.

private

    The type member in type *T* is accessible only from within *T*. This is the default accessibility for class and struct members, and so it may be omitted.

protected

    The type member in class *C* is accessible from within *C* or from within a class that derives from *C*.

protected internal

    The type member in class *C* and assembly *A* is accessible from within *C*, from within a class that derives from *C*, or from within *A*. Note that C# has no concept of protected and internal, whereby "a type member in class *C* and assembly *A* is accessible only from within *C*, or from within a class that both derives from *C* and is within *A*."

Note that a type member may be a nested type. Here is an example of using access modifiers:

```
// Assembly1.dll
using System;
public class A {
  private int x=5;
  public void Foo() {Console.WriteLine (x);}
  protected static void Goo() {}
  protected internal class NestedType {}
}
internal class B {
  private void Hoo () {
    A a1 = new A (); // ok
    Console.WriteLine(a1.x); // error, A.x is private
    A.NestedType n; // ok, A.NestedType is internal
    A.Goo(); // error, A's Goo is protected
  }
}

// Assembly2.exe (references Assembly1.dll)
using System;
```

```
class C : A { // C defaults to internal
  static void Main() { // Main defaults to private
    A a1 = new A(); // ok
    a1.Foo(); // ok
    C.Goo(); // ok, inherits A's protected static member
    new A.NestedType(); // ok, A.NestedType is protected
    new B(); // error, Assembly 1's B is internal
    Console.WriteLine(x); // error, A's x is private
  }
}
```

Restrictions on Access Modifiers

A type or type member cannot declare itself to be more accessible than any of the types it uses in the declaration. For instance, a class cannot be public if it derives from an internal class, or a method cannot be protected if the type of one of its parameters is internal to the assembly. The rationale behind this restriction is that whatever is accessible to another type is actually usable by that type.

In addition, access modifiers cannot be used when they conflict with the purpose of inheritance modifiers. For example, a virtual (or abstract) member cannot be declared private, since it would be impossible to override. Similarly, a sealed class cannot define new protected members, since there is no class that could benefit from this accessibility.

Finally, to maintain the contract of a base class, a function member with the override modifier must have the same accessibility as the virtual member it overrides.

Structs

A struct is similar to a class, with the following major differences:

- A class is a reference type, while a struct is a value type. Consequently, structs are typically used to express simple types, in which value-type semantics are desirable (e.g., an assignment copies a value rather than a reference).

- A class fully supports inheritance, whereas a struct can inherit only from an object and is implicitly sealed (in the runtime, structs actually inherit from `System.ValueType`). Both classes and structs can implement interfaces.

- A class can have a destructor, and a struct cannot.

- A class can define a custom parameterless constructor and initialize instance fields, while a struct cannot. The default parameterless constructor for a struct initializes each field with a default value (effectively zero). If a struct declares a constructor(s), then all of its fields must be assigned in that constructor call.

Here is a simple struct declaration:

```
struct Point {
  public int x, y;
}
```

To create a struct, you can use the new operator, which will initialize all the struct members to their defaults (zero in the case of x and y). If you do not use the new operator, you will need to initialize the struct members yourself. You can also use array declaration syntax to create an array of structs:

```
Point p1 = new Point( );
Point p2;
p2.x = p2.y = 0;
Point[] points = new Point[3];
```

Interfaces

An interface is similar to a class, but with the following major differences:

- An interface provides a specification rather than an implementation for its members. This is similar to a pure abstract class, which consists only of abstract members.

- A class and struct can implement multiple interfaces, while a class can inherit only from a single class.

- A struct can implement an interface, but a struct cannot inherit from a class.

Polymorphism is described as the ability to perform the same operations on many types, as long as each type shares a common subset of characteristics. The purpose of an interface is precisely for defining such a set of characteristics.

An interface is comprised of a set of the following members:

- Method
- Property
- Indexer
- Event

These members are always implicitly public and implicitly abstract (and therefore virtual and nonstatic).

Defining an Interface

An interface declaration is like a class declaration, but it provides no implementation for its members since all its members are implicitly abstract. These members are intended to be implemented by a class or struct that implements the interface. Here is a very simple interface that defines a single method:

```
public interface IDelete {
    void Delete();
}
```

Implementing an Interface

Classes or structs that implement an interface may be said to "fulfill the contract of the interface." In this example, our IDelete interface can be implemented by GUI controls that support the concept of deleting, such as a TextBox, TreeView, or your own custom GUI control.

```
public class TextBox : IDelete {
  public void Delete() {...}
}
public class TreeView : IDelete {
  public void Delete() {...}
}
```

If a class inherits from a base class, then each interface implemented must appear after the base class:

```
public class TextBox : Control, IDelete {...}
public class TreeView : Control, IDelete {...}
```

Using an Interface

An interface is useful when you need multiple classes to share characteristics not present in a common base class. In addition, an interface is a good way to ensure that these classes provide their own implementation for the interface member, since interface members are implicitly abstract.

The following example assumes a form containing many GUI controls (including some TextBox and TreeView controls), in which the currently focused control is accessed with the ActiveControl property. When a user clicks Delete on a menu item or toolbar button, the example tests to see whether ActiveControl implements IDelete; if so, the example casts it to IDelete to call its Delete method:

```
class MyForm {
  ...
  void DeleteClick() {
    if (ActiveControl is IDelete)
      PerformDelete ((IDelete)ActiveControl);
  }
}
```

Extending an Interface

Interfaces may extend other interfaces. For instance:

```
ISuperDelete : IDelete {
  bool CanDelete {get;}
  event EventHandler CanDeleteChanged;
}
```

A control implements the CanDelete property to indicate that it has something to delete and is not read-only, and it implements the CanDeleteChanged event to fire an event whenever its CanDelete property changes. This framework allows our application to ghost its Delete menu item and toolbar button when the ActiveControl is unable to delete.

Explicit Interface Implementation

If there is a name collision between an interface member and an existing member in the class or struct, C# allows you to implement an interface member explicitly to resolve the conflict. In this example, we resolve a conflict when implementing two interfaces that both define a Delete method:

```
public interface IDesignTimeControl {
    ...
    object Delete();
}
public class TextBox : IDelete, IDesignTimeControl {
    ...
    void IDelete.Delete() {}
    object IDesignTimeControl.Delete() {...}
    // Note that explicitly implementing just one of them
    // would be enough to resolve the conflict
}
```

Unlike implicit interface implementations, explicit interface implementations can't be declared with abstract, virtual, override, or new modifiers. In addition, while an implicit implementation requires the use of the public modifier, an explicit implementation has no access modifier. However, to access the method, the class or struct must be cast to the appropriate interface first:

```
TextBox tb = new TextBox();
IDesignTimeControl idtc = (IDesignTimeControl)tb;
IDelete id = (IDelete)lb;
idtc.Delete();
id.Delete();
```

Reimplementing an Interface

If a base class implements an interface member with the virtual (or abstract) modifier, then a derived class can override it. If not, the derived class must reimplement the interface to override that member:

```
public class RichTextBox : TextBox, IDelete {
    // TextBox's IDelete.Delete is not virtual
(since
    // explicit interface implementations cannot
    // be virtual)
    public void Delete() {}
}
```

This lets us use a RichTextBox as an IDelete and calls RichTextBox's version of Delete.

Interface Conversions

A class or struct *T* may be implicitly cast to an interface *I* that *T* implements. Similarly, an interface *X* may be implicitly cast to an interface *Y* from which *X* inherits. An interface may be cast explicitly to any other interface or nonsealed class. However, an explicit cast from an interface *I* to a sealed class or struct *T* is permitted only if it is possible that *T* could implement *I*. For example:

```
interface IDelete {...}
interface IDesigntimeControl {...}
class TextBox : IDelete, IDesignTimeControl {...}
sealed class Timer : IDesignTimeControl {...}

TextBox tb1 = new TextBox ();
IDelete d = tb1; // implicit cast
IDesignTimeControl dtc = (IDesignTimeControl)d;
TextBox tb2 = (TextBox)dtc;
Timer t = (Timer)d; // illegal, a Timer can never
implement IDelete
```

Standard boxing conversions happen when converting between structs and interfaces (see "Boxing and unboxing value types," earlier in this book).

Enums

Enums specify a group of named numeric constants:

```
public enum Direction {North, East, West, South}
```

Unlike in C, enum members must be used with the enum type name. This resolves naming conflicts and makes code clearer:

```
Direction walls = Direction.East;
```

By default, enums are assigned integer constants 0, 1, 2, etc. You may optionally specify an alternative numeric type to base your enum and explicitly specify values for each enum member:

```
[Flags]
public enum Direction : byte {
    North=1, East=2, West=4, South=8
}
Direction walls = Direction.North | Direction.West;
if((walls & Direction.North) != 0)
    System.Console.WriteLine("Can't go north!");
```

The [Flags] attribute is optional and informs the runtime that the values in the enum can be bit-combined and should be decoded accordingly in the debugger or when outputting text to the console. For example:

```
Console.WriteLine(walls); // Displays "North, West"
Console.WriteLine((int) walls); // Displays "5"
```

The System.Enum type also provides many useful static methods for enums that let you determine the underlying type of an enum, check if a specific value is supported, initialize an enum from a string constant, retrieve a list of the valid values, and other common operations such as conversions. Here is an example of the usage:

```
using System;
public enum Toggle : byte { Off=0, On=1 }
class Test {
  static void Main() {
    Type t = Enum.GetUnderlyingType(typeof(Toggle));
    Console.WriteLine(t); // Prints "Byte"

    bool bDimmed = Enum.IsDefined(typeof(Toggle),
                                  "Dimmed");
    Console.WriteLine(bDimmed); // Prints "False"
```

```
Toggle tog =(Toggle)Enum.Parse(typeof(Toggle), "On");
Console.WriteLine(Enum.Format(typeof(Toggle), tog,
                  "D")); // Prints "1"
Console.WriteLine(tog); // Prints "On"

Array oa = Enum.GetValues(typeof(Toggle));
foreach(Toggle toggle in oa) // Prints "On=1, Off=0"
  Console.WriteLine("{0}={1}", toggle,
                    Enum.Format(typeof(Toggle),
                                toggle, "D"));
  }
}
```

Enum Operators

The operators relevant to enums are as follows:

```
==   !=   <   >   <=   >=   +   -   ^   &   |   ~
=    +=   -=   ++  --   sizeof
```

Enum Conversions

Enums may be converted explicitly to other enums. Enums and numeric types may be converted explicitly to one another. A special case is the numeric literal 0, which may be implicitly converted to an enum.

Delegates

A *delegate* is a type defining a method signature, so that delegate instances can hold and invoke a method or list of methods that match its signature. A delegate declaration consists of a name and a method signature. For example:

```
using System;
delegate bool Filter (string s);

class Test {
   static void Main() {
      Filter f = new Filter(FirstHalfOfAlphabet);
      Display(new String [] {"Ant","Lion","Yak"}, f);
   }
```

```
    static bool FirstHalfOfAlphabet(string s) {
        return "N".CompareTo(s) > 0;
    }
    static void Display(string[] names, Filter f) {
        int count = 0;
        foreach(string s in names)
            if(f(s)) // invoke delegate
                Console.WriteLine("Item {0} is {1}", count++,
                                                     s);
    }
}
```

Note that the signature of a delegate method includes its
return type. It also allows the use of a params modifier in its
parameter list, which expands the list of elements that char-
acterize an ordinary method signature. The actual name of
the target method is irrelevant to the delegate.

Multicast Delegates

Delegates can hold and invoke multiple methods. In this
example, we declare a very simple delegate called Method-
Invoker, which we use to hold and then invoke the Foo and
Goo methods sequentially. The += method creates a new delegate by adding the right delegate operand to the left delegate
operand:

```
using System;
delegate void MethodInvoker();
class Test {
    static void Main() {
        new Test(); // prints "Foo","Goo"
    }
    Test () {
        MethodInvoker m = null;
        m += new MethodInvoker(Foo);
        m += new MethodInvoker(Goo);
        m();
    }
    void Foo() {
        Console.WriteLine("Foo");
    }
    void Goo() {
```

```
      Console.WriteLine("Goo");
   }
}
```

A delegate can also be removed from another delegate using the -= operator:

```
Test() {
   MethodInvoker m = null;
   m += new MethodInvoker(Foo);
   m -= new MethodInvoker(Foo);
   // m is now null
}
```

Delegates are invoked in the order they are added. If a delegate has a nonvoid return type, then the value of the last delegate invoked is returned. Note that the += and -= operations on a delegate are not thread-safe. (For more information on threads, see "Threading" in the .NET Framework SDK Documentation.)

Events

Event handling is essentially a process in which one object can notify other objects that an event has occurred. This process is largely encapsulated by multicast delegates, which have this ability built in.

Defining a Delegate for an Event

The .NET Framework provides many event-handling delegates, but you can write your own. For example:

```
public delegate void MoveEventHandler(object source,
MoveEventArgs e);
```

By convention, the delegate's first parameter denotes the source of the event, and the delegate's second parameter derives from System.EventArgs and contains data about the event.

Storing Data for an Event with EventArgs

The EventArgs class may be derived from to include information relevant to a particular event:

```
using System;
public class MoveEventArgs : EventArgs {
  public int newPosition;
  public bool cancel;
  public MoveEventArgs(int newPosition) {
    this.newPosition = newPosition;
  }
}
```

Declaring and Firing an Event

A class or struct can declare an event by applying the event modifier to a delegate field. In this example, the slider class has a Position property that fires a Move event whenever its Position changes:

```
public class Slider {
  int position;
  public event MoveEventHandler Move;
  public int Position {
    get { return position; }
    set {
      if (position != value) { // if position changed
        if (Move != null) { // if invocation list not
                            // empty
          MoveEventArgs args = new MoveEventArgs(value);
          Move(this, args); // fire event
          if (args.cancel)
            return;
        }
        position = value;
      }
    }
  }
}
```

The event keyword promotes encapsulation by ensuring that only the += and -= operations can be performed on the delegate. Other classes may act on the event, but only the Slider can invoke the delegate (fire the event) or clear the delegate's invocation list.

Acting on an Event with an Event Handler

We are able to act on an event by adding an event handler to it. An event handler is a delegate that wraps the method we want invoked when the event is fired.

In this example, we want our Form to act on changes made to a Slider's Position. This is done by creating a MoveEvent-Handler delegate that wraps our event-handling method (the slider_Move method). This delegate is added to the Move event's existing list of MoveEventHandlers (which is initially empty). Changing the position on the slider fires the Move event, which invokes our slider_Move method:

```
using System;
class Form {
  static void Main() {
    Slider slider = new Slider();
    // register with the Move event
    slider.Move += new MoveEventHandler(slider_Move);
    slider.Position = 20;
    slider.Position = 60;
  }
  static void slider_Move(object source, MoveEventArgs e)
{
    if(e.newPosition < 50)
      Console.WriteLine("OK");
    else {
      e.cancel = true;
      Console.WriteLine("Can't go that high!");
    }
  }
}
```

Typically, the Slider class is extended so that it fires the Move event whenever its Position is changed by a mouse movement, key press, etc.

Event Accessors

Similar to the way properties provide controlled access to
fields, event accessors provide controlled access to an event.
Consider the following field declaration:

```
public event MoveEventHandler Move;
```

Except for the underscore prefix added to the field (to avoid
a name collision), this is semantically identical to this:

```
private MoveEventHandler _Move;
public event MoveEventHandler Move {
  add {
    _Move += value;
  }
  remove {
    _Move -= value;
  }
}
```

The ability to specify a custom implementation of add and
remove handlers for an event allows a class to proxy an event
generated by another class, thus acting as a relay for an event
rather than the generator of that event. Another advantage of
this technique is to eliminate the need to store a delegate as a
field, which can be costly in terms of storage space. For
instance, a class with 100 event fields stores 100 delegate
fields, even though maybe only 4 of those events are actually
assigned. Instead, you can store these delegates in a dictionary and add and remove the delegates from that dictionary
(assuming the dictionary holding 4 elements uses less storage space than 100 delegate references).

Operator Overloading

C# lets you overload operators to work with operands that are custom classes or structs using operators. An operator is a static method with the keyword `operator` preceding the operator to overload (instead of a method name), parameters representing the operands, and return types representing the result of an expression. Table 3 lists the available overloadable operators.

Table 3. Overloadable operators

+	-	!	~	++
--	* (binary only)	/	%	& (binary only)
|	^	<<	>>	==
~=	>	<	>=	<=

Literals that also act as overloadable operators are `true` and `false`.

Implementing Value Equality

A pair of references exhibit referential equality when both references point to the same object. By default, the `==` and `!=` operators will compare two reference-type variables by reference. However, it is occasionally more natural for the `==` and `!=` operators to exhibit value equality, whereby the comparison is based on the value of the objects to which the references point.

Whenever overloading the `==` and `!=` operators, you should always override the virtual `Equals` method to route its functionality to the `==` operator. This allows a class to be used polymorphically (which is essential if you want to take advantage of functionality such as the collection classes). It also provides compatibility with other .NET languages that don't overload operators.

```
using System;
class Note {
  int value;
  public Note(int semitonesFromA) {
    value = semitonesFromA;
  }
  public static bool operator ==(Note x, Note y) {
    return x.value == y.value;
  }
  public static bool operator !=(Note x, Note y) {
    return x.value != y.value;
  }
  public override bool Equals(object o) {
    if(!(o is Note))
      return false;
    return this ==(Note)o;
  }
  public static void Main( ) {
    Note a = new Note(4);
    Note b = new Note(4);
    Object c = a;
    Object d = b;

    // To compare a and b by reference
    Console.WriteLine((object)a ==(object)b); // false

    //To compare a and b by value:
    Console.WriteLine(a == b); // true

    //To compare c and d by reference:
    Console.WriteLine(c == d); // false

    //To compare c and d by value:
```

```
        Console.WriteLine(c.Equals(d)); // true
    }
}
```

Logically Paired Operators

The C# compiler enforces operators that are logical pairs to both be defined. These operators are == !=, < >, and <= >=.

Custom Implicit and Explicit Conversions

As explained in the discussion on types, the rationale behind implicit conversions is that they are guaranteed to succeed and do not lose information during the conversion. Conversely, an explicit conversion is required either when runtime circumstances determines whether the conversion will succeed or if information may be lost during the conversion. You should only use a conversion when the outcome of the conversion is unambiguous. Although you can express a Note as a number (frequency in hertz), some semantic information is lost by allowing this conversion. It's less ambiguous to expose a property called Frequency. However, conversions between numeric types are unambiguous. In this example, we define conversions between a BigInt type and an integer:

```
...
// Convert to integer
public static implicit operator int(BigInt x) {
  return x.toInteger(); // heavy lifting not shown
}

// Convert from int
public static explicit operator BigInt(int x) {
  return new BigInt(x);
}
...

BigInt n =(BigInt) 1024; // explicit conversion
int x = n; // implicit conversion
```

Indirectly Overloadable Operators

The && and || operators are automatically evaluated from & and |, so they do not need to be overloaded. The [ ] operators can be customized with indexers (see the section "Indexers"). The assignment operator = cannot be overloaded, but all other assignment operators are automatically evaluated from their corresponding binary operators (e.g., += is evaluated from +).

Try Statements and Exceptions

The purpose of a try statement is to simplify program execution in exceptional circumstances—typically, an error. A try statement does two things. First, it lets the catch block catch exceptions thrown during the try block's execution. Second, it ensures that execution cannot leave the try block without first executing the finally block. A try block must be followed by a catch block(s), a finally block, or both. The form of a try block looks like this:

```
try {
  ... // exception may be thrown during execution of this
      // function
}
catch (ExceptionA ex) {
  ... // react to exception of type ExceptionA
}
catch (ExceptionB ex) {
  ... // react to exception of type ExceptionB
}
finally {
  ... // code to always run after try block executes, even
if
  ... // an exception is not thrown
}
```

Exceptions

C# exceptions are objects that contain information representing the occurrence of an exceptional program state. When an exceptional state occurs (e.g., a method receives an illegal value), an exception object may be thrown, and the call-stack is unwound until the exception is caught by an exception-handling block. For example:

```csharp
using System;
public class WeightCalculator {
  public static float CalcBMI (float weightKilos,
                               float metersTall) {
    if (metersTall < 0 || metersTall > 3)
      throw new ArgumentException ("Impossible Height",
                                  "metersTall");
    if (metersTall < 0 || weightKilos > 1000)
      throw new ArgumentException ("Impossible Weight",
                                  "weightKilos");
    return weightKilos / (metersTall*metersTall);
  }
}
class Test {
  static void Main () {
    TestIt ();
  }
  static void TestIt () {
    try {
      float bmi = WeightCalculator.CalcBMI (100, 5);
      Console.WriteLine(bmi);
    }
    catch(ArgumentException ex) {
      Console.WriteLine(ex);
    }
    finally {
      Console.WriteLine (
        "Thanks for running the program");
    }
    Console.Read();
  }
}
```

In this example, calling CalcBMI throws an ArgumentException indicating that it's impossible for someone to be 5 meters tall. Execution leaves CalcBMI and returns to the calling method, TestIt (which handles the ArgumentException), and displays the exception to the Console. Next, the finally method is executed, which prints "Thanks for running the program" to the Console. Without our try statement, the call stack would be unwound right back to the Main method, and the program would terminate.

The catch Clause

A catch clause specifies the exception type (including derived types) to catch. An exception must be of type System.Exception or a type that derives from System.Exception. Catching System.Exception provides the widest possible net for catching errors, which is useful if your handling of the error is totally generic, such as an error-logging mechanism. Otherwise, you should catch a more specific exception type to prevent your catch block from dealing with a circumstance it wasn't designed to handle (e.g., an out-of-memory exception).

Omitting the exception variable

Specifying only an exception type without a variable name allows an exception to be caught when we don't need to use the exception instance and merely knowing its type is enough. The previous example can be written like this:

```
catch(ArgumentException) { // don't specify variable
  Console.WriteLine("Couldn't calculate ideal weight!");
}
```

While this is legitimate syntax, it is troublesome, since it assumes a particular cause without inspecting the actual exception that was thrown.

Omitting the catch expression

You may also entirely omit the catch expression. This catches an exception of any type, even types thrown by other non-CLS-compliant languages that are not derived from System.Exception. The previous example could be written like this:

```
catch {
  Console.WriteLine("Couldn't calculate ideal weight!");
}
```

This approach is even more problematic than omitting the exception variable, since it assumes that the calculation is responsible for any and all exceptions and this may not be the case—for example, an exception may arise from within the runtime in response to a grave operating-system error.

Specifying multiple catch clauses

When declaring multiple catch clauses, only the first catch clause with an exception type that matches the thrown exception executes its catch block. It is illegal for an exception type *B* to precede an exception type *D* if *B* is a base class of *D*, since it would be unreachable.

```
try {...}
catch (NullReferenceException) {...}
catch (ArgumentException) {...}
catch {...}
```

The finally Block

A finally block is always executed when control leaves the try block. A finally block is executed at any of the following periods:

- Immediately after the try block completes
- Immediately after the try block prematurely exits with a jump statement (e.g., return, goto) and immediately before the target of the jump statement
- Immediately after a catch block executes

finally blocks can add determinism to a program's execution by ensuring that the specified code always gets executed.

In our main example, if the height passed to the calculator is invalid, an ArgumentException that executes the catch block is thrown, followed by the finally block. However, if anything else goes wrong, the finally block is still executed. This ensures that we say goodbye to our user before exiting the program.

Key Properties of System.Exception

Notable properties of System.Exception include the following:

StackTrace
> A string representing all the methods that are called from the origin of the exception to the catch block.

Message
> A string with a description of the error.

InnerException
> A cascading exception structure that can be particularly useful when debugging. Sometimes it is useful to catch an exception, then throw a new, more specific exception. For instance, we may catch an IOException and then throw a ProblemFooingException that contains more specific information on what went wrong. In this scenario, the ProblemFooingException should include the IOException as the InnerException argument in its constructor, which is assigned to the InnerException property.

NOTE

Note that in C# all exceptions are runtime exceptions—there is no equivalent to Java's compile-time checked exceptions.

Attributes

Attributes are language constructs that can decorate a code element (assemblies, modules, types, members, return values, and parameters) with additional information.

In every language, you specify information associated with the types, methods, parameters, and other elements of your program. For example, a type can specify a list of interfaces from which it derives, or a parameter can specify modifiers, such as the ref modifier in C#. The limitation of this approach is that you can associate information with code elements using only the predefined constructs that the language provides.

Attributes allow programmers to extend the types of information associated with these code elements. For example, serialization in the .NET Framework uses various serialization attributes applied to types and fields to define how these code elements are serialized. This approach is more flexible than requiring the language to have special syntax for serialization.

Attribute Classes

An attribute is defined by a class that inherits (directly or indirectly) from the abstract class System.Attribute. When specifying an attribute to an element, the attribute name is the name of the type. By convention, the derived type name ends in Attribute, although specifying the suffix is not required when specifying the attribute.

In this example, the Foo class is specified as serializable using the Serializable attribute:

```
[Serializable]
public class Foo {...}
```

The Serializable attribute is actually a type declared in the System namespace, as follows:

```
class SerializableAttribute : Attribute {...}
```

We could also specify the Serializable attribute using its fully qualified type name, as follows:

```
[System.SerializableAttribute]
public class Foo {...}
```

The preceding two examples of using the Serializable attribute are semantically identical.

The C# language and the FCL include a number of predefined attributes. For more information about the other attributes included in the FCL and about creating your own attributes, see the "Writing Custom Attributes" topic in the .NET Framework SDK Documentation.

Named and Positional Parameters

Attributes can take parameters, which can specify additional information on the code element beyond the mere presence of the attribute.

In this example, the class Foo is specified as obsolete using the Obsolete attribute. This attribute allows the inclusion of parameters to specify both a message and whether the compiler should treat the use of this class as an error:

```
[Obsolete("Use Bar class instead", IsError=true)]
public class Foo {...}
```

Attribute parameters fall into one of two categories: positional and named. In the preceding example, Use Bar class instead is a positional parameter, and IsError=true is a named parameter.

The positional parameters for an attribute correspond to the parameters passed to the attribute type's public constructors. The named parameters for an attribute correspond to the set of public read-write or write-only instance properties and fields of the attribute type.

When specifying an attribute of an element, positional parameters are mandatory, and named parameters are optional. Since the parameters used to specify an attribute are evaluated at compile time, they are generally limited to constant expressions.

Attribute Targets

Implicitly, the target of an attribute is the code element it immediately precedes, as with the attributes we have covered so far. Sometimes it is necessary to specify explicitly that the attribute applies to particular target.

Here is an example of using the `CLSCompliant` attribute to specify the level of CLS compliance for an entire assembly:

```
[assembly:CLSCompliant(true)]
```

Specifying Multiple Attributes

Multiple attributes can be specified for a single code element. Each attribute can be listed within the same pair of square brackets (separated by a comma), in separate pairs of square brackets, or in any combination of the two.

Consequently, the following three examples are semantically identical:

```
[Serializable, Obsolete, CLSCompliant(false)]
public class Bar {...}

[Serializable]
[Obsolete]
[CLSCompliant(false)]
public class Bar {...}

[Serializable, Obsolete]
[CLSCompliant(false)]
public class Bar {...}
```

Unsafe Code and Pointers

C# supports direct memory manipulation via pointers within blocks of code marked unsafe and compiled with the /unsafe compiler option. Pointer types are primarily useful for interop with C APIs, but may also be used for accessing memory outside the managed heap or for performance-critical hotspots.

Pointer Basics

For every value type or pointer type V, there is a corresponding pointer type V^*. A pointer instance holds the address of a value. This is considered to be of type V, but pointer types can be (unsafely) cast to any other pointer type. Table 4 lists the main pointer operators.

Table 4. Principal pointer operators

Operator	Meaning
&	The address-of operator returns a pointer to the address of a value
*	The dereference operator returns the value at the address of a pointer
->	The pointer-to-member operator is a syntactic shortcut, in which x->y is equivalent to (*x).y

Unsafe Code

By marking a type, type member, or statement block with the unsafe keyword, you're permitted to use pointer types and perform C++-style pointer operations on memory within that scope. Here is an example of using pointers with a managed object:

```
unsafe void RedFilter(int[,] bitmap) {
  int length = bitmap.Length;
  fixed (int* b = bitmap) {
    int* p = b;
    for(int i = 0; i < length; i++)
      *p++ &= 0xFF;
  }
}
```

Unsafe code typically runs faster than a corresponding safe implementation, which in this case requires a nested loop with array indexing and bounds checking. An unsafe C# method may also be faster than calling an external C function, since there is no overhead associated with leaving the managed execution environment. You must compile unsafe code with the /unsafe compiler switch.

The fixed Statement

The fixed statement is required to pin a managed object, such as the bitmap in the previous example. During the execution of a program, many objects are allocated and deallocated from the heap. In order to avoid unnecessary waste or fragmentation of memory, the garbage collector moves objects around. Pointing to an object is futile if its address could change while referencing it, so the fixed statement tells the garbage collector to "pin" the object and not move it around. This may have an impact on the efficiency of the runtime, so fixed blocks should be used only briefly, and heap allocation should be avoided within the fixed block.

C# returns a pointer only from a value type, and never directly from a reference type. Syntactically, arrays and strings are an exception to this, since they actually return a pointer to their first element (which must be a value type), rather than the objects themselves.

Value types declared inline within reference types require the reference type to be pinned, as follows:

```
class Test {
  int x;
  static void Main() {
    Test test = new Test ();
    unsafe {
      fixed(int* p = &test.x) { // pins test
        *p = 9;
      }
      System.Console.WriteLine(test.x);
    }
  }
}
```

The Pointer-to-Member Operator

In addition to the & and * operators, C# also provides the C++-style -> operator, which can be used on structs:

```
struct Test {
  int x;
  unsafe static void Main() {
    Test test = new Test();
    Test* p = &test;
    p->x = 9;
```

```
        System.Console.WriteLine(test.x);
    }
}
```

The stackalloc Keyword

Memory can be allocated explicitly in a block on the stack using the stackalloc keyword. Since it is allocated on the stack, its lifetime is limited to the execution of the method, just as with any other local variable. The block may use [ ] indexing, but is purely a value type with no additional self-describing information or bounds-checking that an array provides.

```
unsafe {
  int* a = stackalloc int [10];
  for (int i = 0; i < 10; ++i)
    Console.WriteLine(a[i]); // print raw memory
}
```

Void*

Rather than pointing to a specific value type, a pointer may make no assumptions about the type of the underlying data. This approach is useful for functions that deal with raw memory. An implicit conversion exists from any pointer type to a void*. A void* cannot be dereferenced, and arithmetic operations cannot be performed on void pointers. For example:

```
class Test {
  unsafe static void Main () {
    short[ ] a = {1,1,2,3,5,8,13,21,34,55};
      fixed (short* p = a) {
        // sizeof returns size of value-type in bytes
        Zap (p, a.Length * sizeof (short));
      }
    foreach (short x in a)
      System.Console.WriteLine (x); // prints all zeros
  }
  unsafe static void Zap (void* memory, int byteCount) {
    byte* b = (byte*)memory;
      for (int i = 0; i < byteCount; i++)
        *b++ = 0;
  }
}
```

Pointers to Unmanaged Code

Pointers are also useful for accessing data outside the managed heap (such as when interacting with C DLLs or COM) or when dealing with data not in the main memory (such as graphics memory or a storage medium on an embedded device).

Preprocessor Directives

Preprocessor directives supply the compiler with additional information about regions of code. The most common preprocessor directives are the conditional directives, which provide a way to include or exclude regions of code from compilation. For example:

```
#define DEBUG
using System;
class MyClass {
  static int x = 5;
  static void Main() {
  # if DEBUG
    Console.WriteLine("Testing: x = {0}", x);
  # endif
  }
}
```

In this class, the statement in Foo is compiled as conditionally dependent upon the presence of the DEBUG symbol. If we remove the DEBUG symbol, the statement is not compiled. Preprocessor symbols can be defined within a source file (as we have done) and can be passed to the compiler with the /define: symbol command-line option.

The #error and #warning symbols prevent accidental misuse of conditional directives by making the compiler generate a warning or error when given an undesirable set of compilation symbols. See Table 5 for a list of preprocessor directives and their actions.

Table 5. Preprocessor directives

Preprocessor directive	Action
#define *symbol*	Defines *symbol*
#undef *symbol*	Undefines *symbol*
#if *symbol* [*operator symbol2*] ...	*symbol* to test; *operator*s are ==, !=, &&, and ||, followed by #else, #elif, and #endif
#else	Executes code to subsequent #endif
#elif *symbol* [*operator symbol2*]	Combines #else branch and #if test
#endif	Ends conditional directives
#warning *text*	*text* of the warning to appear in compiler output
#error *text*	*text* of the error to appear in compiler output
#line *number* ["*file*"]	*number* specifies the line in source code; *file* is the filename to appear in computer output
#region *name*	Marks the beginning of outline
#endregion	Ends an outline region

Framework Class Library Overview

Almost all the capabilities of the .NET Framework are exposed via a set of managed types known as the Framework Class Library (FCL). Because these types are CLS compliant, they are accessible from almost any .NET language. FCL types are grouped logically by namespace and are exported from a set of assemblies that are part of the .NET platform. Using these types in a C# application requires you to reference the appropriate assembly when compiling (most essential assemblies are referenced by default; see "Namespaces and Assemblies" later in this book). For you to work effectively in C# on the .NET platform, it is important to understand the general capabilities in the predefined class library.

In this section, we give an overview of the entire FCL (broken down by logical area) and provide references to relevant types and namespaces so that you can explore their details in the .NET Framework SDK on your own.

The specific types and namespaces mentioned in this overview are based on the final released version of the .NET Framework.

Useful tools for exploring the FCL include the .NET Framework SDK documentation, the Visual Studio .NET documentation, the *WinCV.exe* class browser, and the *ILDasm.exe* disassembler.

Core Types

The core types are contained in the System namespace. This namespace is the heart of the FCL and contains classes, interfaces, and attributes on which all other types depend. The root of the FCL is the type Object, from which all other .NET types derive. Other fundamental types are ValueType (the base type for structs), Enum (the base type for enums), Convert (used to convert between base types), Exception (the base type for all exceptions), and the boxed versions of the predefined value types. Interfaces that are used throughout the FCL (such as ICloneable, IComparable, IFormattable, and IConvertible) are also defined here. Extended types such as DateTime, TimeSpan, and DBNull are available as well. Other classes include support for delegates (see "Delegates" earlier in this book), basic math operations, custom attributes (see the earlier section "Attributes"), and exception handling (see the earlier "Try Statements and Exceptions").

For more information, see the System namespace in the .NET Framework SDK Documentation.

Text

The FCL provides rich support for text. Important types include the System.String class for handling immutable strings, a `StringBuilder` class that provides string-handling operations with support for locale-aware comparison operations and multiple string-encoding formats (ASCII, Unicode, UTF-7, and UTF-8), as well as a set of classes that provide regular-expression support.

For more information, see the following namespaces in the .NET Framework SDK Documentation.

```
System.Text
System.Text.RegularExpressions
```

An important related type in another namespace is `System.String`.

Collections

The FCL provides a set of general-purpose data structures such as `System.Array`, `ArrayList`, `Hashtable`, `Queue`, `Stack`, `BitArray`, and more. Standardized design patterns using common base types and public interfaces allow consistent handling of collections throughout the FCL for both predefined and user-defined collection types.

For more information, see the following namespaces:

```
System.Collections
System.Collections.Specialized
```

An important related type in another namespace is `System.Array`.

Streams and I/O

The FCL provides good support for accessing the standard input, output, and error streams. Classes are also provided for performing binary and text file I/O, registering for notification of filesystem events, and accessing a secure user-specific storage area known as Isolated Storage.

For more information, see the following namespaces:

```
System.IO
System.IO.IsolatedStorage
```

An important related type in another namespace is `System.Console`.

Networking

The FCL provides a layered set of classes for communicating over the network using different levels of abstraction, including raw socket access; TCP, UDP, and HTTP protocol support; a high-level request/response mechanism based on URIs and streams; and pluggable protocol handlers.

For more information, see the following namespaces:

```
System.Net
System.Net.Sockets
```

An important related type in the `System.IO` namespace is the `Stream` class.

Threading

The FCL provides rich support for building multithreaded applications, including thread and thread-pool management, thread-synchronization mechanisms (such as monitors, mutexes, events, reader/writer locks, etc.), and access to such underlying platform features as I/O completion ports and system timers.

For more information, see the following namespaces:

```
System.Threading
System.Timers
```

Important related types in other namespaces include `System.Thread` and `System.ThreadStaticAttribute`.

Security

The FCL provides classes for manipulating all elements of the .NET Framework's Code Access Security model, including security policies, security principals, permission sets, and evidence. These classes also support cryptographic algorithms such as DES, 3DES, RC2, RSA, DSig, MD5, SHA1, and Base64 encoding for stream transformations.

For more information, see the following namespaces:

```
System.Security
System.Security.Cryptography
System.Security.Cryptography.X509Certificates
System.Security.Cryptography.Xml
System.Security.Permissions
System.Security.Policy
System.Security.Principal
```

Reflection and Metadata

The .NET runtime depends heavily on the existence of metadata and the ability to inspect and manipulate it dynamically. The FCL exposes this via a set of abstract classes that mirror the significant elements of an application (assemblies, modules, types, and members) and provide support for creating instances of FCL types and new types on the fly.

For more information, see the following namespaces:

```
System.Reflection
System.Reflection.Emit
```

Important related types in other namespaces include System. Type, System.Activator and System.AppDomain.

Assemblies

The FCL provides attributes that tag the metadata on an assembly with information such as target OS and processor, assembly version, and other information. The FCL also provides classes to manipulate assemblies, modules, and assembly strong names.

For more information, see the following namespace:

```
System.Reflection
```

Serialization

The FCL includes support for serializing arbitrary object graphs to and from a stream. This serialization can store and transmit complex data structures via files or the network. The default serializers provide binary and XML-based formatting but can be extended with user-defined formatters.

For more information, see the following namespaces:

```
System.Runtime.Serialization
System.Runtime.Serialization.Formatters
System.Runtime.Serialization.Formatters.Soap
System.Runtime.Serialization.Formatters.Binary
```

Important related types in other namespaces include System.NonSerializedAttribute and System.SerializableAttribute.

Remoting

Remoting is the cornerstone of a distributed application, and the FCL provides excellent support for making and receiving remote method calls. Calls may be synchronous or asynchronous, support request/response or one-way modes, delivered over multiple transports (TCP, HTTP, and SMTP), and serialized in multiple formats (SOAP and binary). The remoting infrastructure supports multiple activation models, lease-based object lifetimes, distributed object identity, object marshaling by reference and by value, and message interception. These types can be extended with user-defined channels, serializers, proxies, and call context.

For more information, see the following namespaces:

```
System.Runtime.Remoting
System.Runtime.Remoting.Activation
System.Runtime.Remoting.Channels
System.Runtime.Remoting.Channels.Http
System.Runtime.Remoting.Channels.Tcp
System.Runtime.Remoting.Contexts
System.Runtime.Remoting.Lifetime
System.Runtime.Remoting.Messaging
```

```
System.Runtime.Remoting.Metadata
System.Runtime.Remoting.MetadataServices
System.Runtime.Remoting.Proxies
System.Runtime.Remoting.Services
```

Important related types in other namespaces include System.
AppDomain, System.ContextBoundObject, System.Context-
StaticAttribute, and System.MarshalByRefObject.

Web Services

Logically, web services are simply another form of remoting.
In reality, the FCL support for web services is considered
part of ASP.NET and is entirely separate from the CLR
remoting infrastructure. Classes and attributes exist for
describing and publishing web services, discovering what
web services are exposed at a particular endpoint (URI), and
invoking a web service method.

For more information, see the following namespaces:

```
System.Web.Services
System.Web.Services.Configuration
System.Web.Services.Description
System.Web.Services.Discovery
System.Web.Services.Protocols
```

Data Access

The FCL includes a set of classes that access data sources
and manage complex data sets. Known as ADO.NET, these
classes are the managed replacement for ADO under Win32.
ADO.NET supports both connected and disconnected operations, multiple data providers (including nonrelational data
sources), and serialization to and from XML.

For more information, see the following namespaces:

```
System.Data
System.Data.Common
System.Data.OleDb
System.Data.SqlClient
System.Data.SqlTypes
```

XML

The FCL provides broad support for XML 1.0, XML schemas, XML namespaces with two separate XML parsing models (a DOM2-based model and a pull-mode variant of SAX2), and implementations of XSLT, XPath, and SOAP 1.1.

For more information, see the following namespaces:

```
System.Xml
System.Xml.Schema
System.Xml.Serialization
System.Xml.XPath
System.Xml.Xsl
```

Graphics

The FCL includes classes to support working with graphic images. Known as GDI+, these classes are the managed equivalent of GDI under Win32 and include support for brushes, fonts, bitmaps, text rendering, drawing primitives, image conversions, and print-preview capabilities.

For more information, see the following namespaces:

```
System.Drawing
System.Drawing.Design
System.Drawing.Drawing2D
System.Drawing.Imaging
System.Drawing.Printing
System.Drawing.Text
```

Rich Client Applications

The FCL includes support for creating classic GUI applications. This support is known as Windows Forms and consists of a forms package, a predefined set of GUI components, and a component model suited to RAD designer tools. These classes provide varying degrees of abstraction from low-level message-loop handler classes to high-level layout managers and visual inheritance.

For more information, see the following namespaces:

```
System.Windows.Forms
System.Windows.Forms.Design
```

Web-Based Applications

The FCL includes support for creating web-based applications. This support is known as Web Forms and consists of a server-side forms package that generates HTML UI, a predefined set of HTML-based GUI widgets, and a component model suited to RAD designer tools. The FCL also includes a set of classes that manage session state, security, caching, debugging, tracing, localization, configuration, and deployment for web-based applications. Finally, the FCL includes the classes and attributes that produce and consume web services, which are described earlier in the "Web Services" section. Collectively, these capabilities are known as ASP.NET and are a complete replacement for ASP under Win32.

For more information, see the following namespaces:

```
System.Web
System.Web.Caching
System.Web.Configuration
System.Web.Hosting
System.Web.Mail
System.Web.Security
System.Web.SessionState
System.Web.UI
System.Web.UI.Design
System.Web.UI.Design.WebControls
System.Web.UI.HtmlControls
System.Web.UI.WebControls
```

Globalization

The FCL provides classes that aid globalization by supporting code-page conversions, locale-aware string operations, date/time conversions, and the use of resource files to centralize localization work.

For more information, see the following namespaces:

```
System.Globalization
System.Resources
```

Configuration

The FCL provides access to the .NET configuration system, which includes a per-user and per-application configuration model with inheritance of configuration settings, and a transacted installer framework. Classes exist both to use the configuration framework and to extend it.

For more information, see the following namespaces:

```
System.Configuration
System.Configuration.Assemblies
System.Configuration.Install
```

Advanced Component Services

The FCL provides support for building on COM+ services such as distributed transactions, JIT activation, object pooling, queuing, and events. The FCL also includes types that provide access to reliable, asynchronous, one-way messaging via an existing Message Queue infrastructure (MSMQ), in addition to classes that provide access to existing directory services (Active Directory).

For more information, see the following namespaces:

```
System.DirectoryServices
System.EnterpriseServices
System.EnterpriseServices.CompensatingResourceManager
System.Messaging
```

Diagnostics and Debugging

The FCL includes classes that provide debug tracing with multilistener support, access to the event log, access to process, thread, and stack frame information, and the ability to create and consume performance counters.

For more information, see the following namespaces:

```
System.Diagnostics
System.Diagnostics.SymbolStore
```

Interoperating with Unmanaged Code

The .NET runtime supports bidirectional interop with unmanaged code via COM, COM+, and native Win32 API calls. The FCL provides a set of classes and attributes that support this, including precise control of managed object lifetime and the option of creating user-defined custom marshallers to handle specific interop situations.

For more information, see the following namespaces:

```
System.Runtime.InteropServices
System.Runtime.InteropServices.CustomMarshalers
System.Runtime.InteropServices.Expando
```

An important related type in another namespace is System.Buffer.

Compiler and Tool Support

In the .NET runtime, components are distinguished from classes by the presence of additional metadata and other apparatus that facilitate the use of the component forms packages such as Windows Forms and Web Forms. The FCL provides classes and attributes that support both the creation of components and the creation of tools that consume components. These classes also include the ability to generate and compile C#, JScript, and VB.NET source code.

For more information, see the following namespaces:

```
Microsoft.CSharp
Microsoft.JScript
Microsoft.VisualBasic
Microsoft.Vsa
System.CodeDom
System.CodeDom.Compiler
System.ComponentModel
```

```
System.ComponentModel.Design
System.ComponentModel.Design.Serialization
System.Runtime.CompilerServices
```

Runtime Facilities

The FCL provides classes that can control runtime behavior. The canonical examples are the classes that control the garbage collector and those that provide strong and weak reference support.

For more information, see the following namespace:

```
System
```

An important related type in another namespace is System.Runtime.InteropServices.GCHandle.

Native OS Facilities

The FCL gives support for controlling existing NT services and creating new ones. It also provides access to certain native Win32 facilities such as the Windows registry and the Windows Management Instrumentation (WMI).

For more information, see the following namespaces:

```
Microsoft.Win32
System.Management
System.Management.Instrumentation
System.ServiceProcess
```

Namespaces and Assemblies

Table 6 allows you to look up a namespace and determine which assemblies export that namespace. This information is helpful when constructing the appropriate /reference:<file list> command-line option for the C# compiler. However, commonly used assemblies are referenced by default.

For a complete list of default assemblies, see the global C# response file, *csc.rsp*, in *%SystemRoot%\Microsoft.NET*

Framework\VERSION, where *VERSION* is the version number of the framework (the first release of .NET is v1.0.3705). You can modify *csc.rsp* to affect all compilations that run on your machine, or you can create a local *csc.rsp* in your current directory. The local response file is processed after the global one. You can use the /noconfig switch with *csc.exe* to disable the local and global *csc.rsp* files entirely.

Table 6. Namespace and assembly cross-reference

Namespace	DLLs
Accessibility	*Accessibility.dll*
EnvDTE	*envdte.dll*
IEHost.Execute	*IEExecRemote.dll*
Microsoft.CLRAdmin	*mscorcfg.dll*
Microsoft.CSharp	*cscompmgd.dll* *System.dll*
Microsoft.IE	*IEHost.dll* *IIEHost.dll*
Microsoft.JScript	*Microsoft.JScript.dll*
Microsoft.JScript.Vsa	*Microsoft.JScript.dll*
Microsoft.Office.Core	*office.dll*
Microsoft.VisualBasic	*Microsoft.VisualBasic.dll* *System.dll*
Microsoft.VisualBasic.Compatibility.VB6	*Microsoft.VisualBasic.Compatibility.Data.dll* *Microsoft.VisualBasic.Compatibility.dll*
Microsoft.VisualBasic.CompilerServices	*Microsoft.VisualBasic.dll*
Microsoft.VisualBasic.Vsa	*Microsoft.VisualBasic.Vsa.dll*
Microsoft.VisualC	*Microsoft.VisualC.dll*
Microsoft.Vsa	*Microsoft.JScript.dll* *Microsoft.Vsa.dll*
Microsoft.Vsa.Vb.CodeDOM	*Microsoft.Vsa.Vb.CodeDOMProcessor. dll*
Microsoft.Win32	*mscorlib.dll* *System.dll*
Microsoft_VsaVb	*Micsoroft._VsaVb.dll*

Table 6. Namespace and assembly cross-reference (continued)

Namespace	DLLs
RegCode	RegCode.dll
System	mscorlib.dll System.dll
System.CodeDom	System.dll
System.CodeDom.Compiler	System.dll
System.Collections	mscorlib.dll
System.Collections.Specialized	System.dll
System.ComponentModel	System.dll
System.ComponentModel.Design	System.Design.dll System.dll
System.ComponentModel.Design. Serialization	System.Design.dll System.dll
System.Configuration	System.dll
System.Configuration.Assemblies	mscorlib.dll
System.Configuration.Install	System.Configuration.Install.dll
System.Data	System.Data.dll
System.Data.Common	System.Data.dll
System.Data.OleDb	System.Data.dll
System.Data.SqlClient	System.Data.dll
System.Data.SqlTypes	System.Data.dll
System.Diagnostics	mscorlib.dll System.Configuration.Install.dll
System.Diagnostics	mscorlib.dll System.Configuration.Install.dll
System.Diagnostics.Design	System.Design.dll
System.Diagnostics.SymbolStore	ISymWrapper.dll mscorlib.dll
System.DirectoryServices	System.DirectoryServices.dll
System.Drawing	System.Drawing.dll

Table 6. Namespace and assembly cross-reference (continued)

Namespace	DLLs
System.Drawing.Design	*System.Drawing.Design.dll* *System.Drawing.dll*
System.Drawing.Drawing2D	*System.Drawing.dll*
System.Drawing.Imaging	*System.Drawing.dll*
System.Drawing.Printing	*System.Drawing.dll*
System.Drawing.Text	*System.Drawing.dll*
System.EnterpriseServices	*System.EnterpriseServices.dll*
System.EnterpriseServices.CompensatingResourceManager	*System.EnterpriseServices.dll*
System.EnterpriseServices.Internal	*System.EnterpriseServices.dll*
System.Globalization	*mscorlib.dll*
System.IO	*mscorlib.dll* *System.dll*
System.IO.IsolatedStorage	*mscorlib.dll*
System.Management	*System.Management.dll*
System.Management.Instrumentation	*System.Management.dll*
System.Messaging	*System.Messaging.dll*
System.Messaging.Design	*System.Design.dll* *System.Messaging.dll*
System.Net	*System.dll*
System.Net.Sockets	*System.dll*
System.Reflection	*mscorlib.dll*
System.Reflection.Emit	*mscorlib.dll*
System.Resources	*mscorlib.dll* *System.Windows.Forms.dll*
System.Runtime.CompilerServices	*mscorlib.dll*
System.Runtime.InteropServices	*mscorlib.dll*

Table 6. Namespace and assembly cross-reference (continued)

Namespace	DLLs
System.Runtime. InteropServices. CustomMarshalers	*CustomMarshalers.dll*
System.Runtime. InteropServices.Expando	*mscorlib.dll*
System.Runtime.Remoting	*mscorlib.dll*
System.Runtime.Remoting. Activation	*mscorlib.dll*
System.Runtime.Remoting. Channels	*mscorlib.dll* *System.Runtime.Remoting.dll*
System.Runtime.Remoting. Channels.Http	*System.Runtime.Remoting.dll*
System.Runtime.Remoting. Channels.Tcp	*System.Runtime.Remoting.dll*
System.Runtime.Remoting. Contexts	*mscorlib.dll*
System.Runtime.Remoting. Lifetime	*mscorlib.dll*
System.Runtime.Remoting. Messaging	*mscorlib.dll*
System.Runtime.Remoting. Metadata	*mscorlib.dll*
System.Runtime.Remoting. Metadata. W3cXsd2001	*mscorlib.dll*
System.Runtime.Remoting. MetadataServices	*System.Runtime.Remoting.dll*
System.Runtime.Remoting. Proxies	*mscorlib.dll*
System.Runtime.Remoting. Services	*mscorlib.dll* *System.Runtime.Remoting.dll*
System.Runtime. Serialization	*mscorlib.dll*
System.Runtime. Serialization.Formatters	*mscorlib.dll*

Table 6. Namespace and assembly cross-reference (continued)

Namespace	DLLs
System.Runtime. Serialization.Formatters. Binary	*mscorlib.dll*
System.Runtime. Serialization.Formatters. Soap	*System.Runtime.Serialization. Formatters.Soap.dll*
System.Security	*mscorlib.dll*
System.Security. Cryptography	*mscorlib.dll*
System.Security. Cryptography. X509Certificates	*mscorlib.dll* *System.dll*
System.Security. Cryptography.Xml	*System.Security.dll*
System.Security.Permissions	*mscorlib.dll* *System.dll*
System.Security.Policy	*mscorlib.dll*
System.Security.Principal	*mscorlib.dll*
System.ServiceProcess	*System.ServiceProcess.dll*
System.ServiceProcess. Design	*System.Design.dll* *System.ServiceProcess.dll*
System.Text	*mscorlib.dll*
System.Text. RegularExpressions	*System.dll*
System.Threading	*mscorlib.dll* *System.dll*
System.Timers	*System.dll*
System.Web	*System.Web.dll*
System.Web.Caching	*System.Web.dll*
System.Web.Configuration	*System.Web.dll*
System.Web.Handlers	*System.Web.dll*
System.Web.Hosting	*System.Web.dll*
System.Web.Mail	*System.Web.dll*

Table 6. Namespace and assembly cross-reference (continued)

Namespace	DLLs
System.Web.RegularExpressions	*System.Web.RegularExpressions.dll*
System.Web.Security	*System.Web.dll*
System.Web.Services	*System.Web.Services.dll*
System.Web.Services.Configuration	*System.Web.Services.dll*
System.Web.Services.Description	*System.Web.Services.dll*
System.Web.Services.Discovery	*System.Web.Services.dll*
System.Web.Services.Protocols	*System.Web.Services.dll*
System.Web.SessionState	*System.Web.dll*
System.Web.UI	*System.Web.dll*
System.Web.UI.Design	*System.Design.dll*
System.Web.UI.Design.WebControls	*System.Design.dll*
System.Web.UI.HtmlControls	*System.Web.dll*
System.Web.UI.WebControls	*System.Web.dll*
System.Web.Util	*System.Web.dll*
System.Windows.Forms	*System.Windows.Forms.dll*
System.Windows.Forms.ComponentModel.Com2Interop	*System.Windows.Forms.dll*
System.Windows.Forms.Design	*System.Design.dll* *System.Windows.Forms.dll*
System.Windows.Forms.PropertyGridInternal	*System.Windows.Forms.dll*
System.Xml	*System.Data.dll* *System.XML.dll*
System.Xml.Schema	*System.XML.dll*
System.Xml.Serialization	*System.XML.dll*
System.Xml.XPath	*System.XML.dll*
System.Xml.Xsl	*System.XML.dll*

Regular Expressions

Tables 7 through 16 summarize the regular-expression grammar and syntax supported by the regular-expression classes in System.Text.RegularExpressions. (For more information, see the ".NET Framework Regular Expressions" topic in the .NET Framework SDK Documentation.) Each of the modifiers and qualifiers in the tables can substantially change the behavior of the matching and searching patterns. For further information on regular expressions, we recommend the definitive *Mastering Regular Expressions* by Jeffrey E. F. Friedl (O'Reilly, 2002).

All the syntax described in the tables should match the Perl5 syntax, with specific exceptions noted.

Table 7 . Character escapes

Escape code sequence	Meaning	Hexadecimal equivalent
\a	Bell	\u0007
\b	Backspace	\u0008
\t	Tab	\u0009
\r	Carriage return	\u000D
\v	Vertical tab	\u000B
\f	Form feed	\u000C
\n	Newline	\u000A
\e	Escape	\u001B
\040	ASCII character as octal	
\x20	ASCII character as hex	
\cC	ASCII control character	
\u0020	Unicode character as hex	
\non-escape	A nonescape character	

As a special case: within a regular expression, \b means word boundary, except in a [ ] set, in which \b means the backspace character.

Table 8. Substitutions

Expression	Meaning
$group-number	Substitutes last substring matched by group-number
${group-name}	Substitutes last substring matched by (?<group-name>)

Substitutions are specified only within a replacement pattern.

Table 9. Character sets

Expression	Meaning
.	Matches any character except \n
[characterlist]	Matches a single character in the list
[^characterlist]	Matches a single character not in the list
[char0-char1]	Matches a single character in a range
\w	Matches a word character; same as [a-zA-Z_0-9]
\W	Matches a nonword character
\s	Matches a space character; same as [\n\r\t\v\f]
\S	Matches a nonspace character
\d	Matches a decimal digit; same as [0-9]
\D	Matches a nondigit

Table 10. Positioning assertions

Expression	Meaning
^	Beginning of line
$	End of line
\A	Beginning of string
\Z	End of line or string
\z	Exactly the end of string
\G	Where search started
\b	On a word boundary
\B	Not on a word boundary

Table 11. Quantifiers

Quantifier	Meaning
*	0 or more matches
+	1 or more matches
?	0 or 1 matches
{*n*}	Exactly *n* matches
{*n*,}	At least *n* matches
{*n*,*m*}	At least *n*, but no more than *m* matches
*?	Lazy *, finds first match that has minimum repeats
+?	Lazy +, minimum repeats, but at least 1
??	Lazy ?, zero or minimum repeats
{*n*}?	Lazy {*n*}, exactly *n* matches
{n,}?	Lazy {*n*}, minimum repeats, but at least *n*
{*n*,*m*}?	Lazy {*n*,*m*}, minimum repeats, but at least *n*, and no more than *m*

Table 12. Grouping constructs

Syntax	Meaning
( )	Capture matched substring
(?<*name*>)	Capture matched substring into group *name*[a]
(?<*name1*-*name2*>)	Undefine *name2*, and store interval and current group into *name1*; if *name2* is undefined, matching backtracks; *name1* is *optional*[a]
(?:)	Noncapturing group
(?imnsx-imnsx:)	Apply or disable matching options
(?=)	Continue matching only if subexpression matches on right
(?!)	Continue matching only if subexpression doesn't match on right
(?<=)	Continue matching only if subexpression matches on left

Table 12. Grouping constructs (continued)

Syntax	Meaning
(?<!)	Continue matching only if subexpression doesn't match on left
(?>)	Subexpression is matched once, but isn't backtracked

a Single quotes may be used instead of angle brackets—for example, (?'name').

NOTE

The named capturing group syntax follows a suggestion made by Jeffrey E. F. Friedl in *Mastering Regular Expressions*. All other grouping constructs use the Perl5 syntax.

Table 13. Back references

Parameter syntax	Meaning
\count	Back reference count occurrences
\k<name>	Named back reference

Table 14. Alternation

Expression syntax	Meaning
|	Logical OR
(?(expression)yes|no)	Matches yes if expression matches, else no; the no is optional
(?(name)yes|no)	Matches yes if named string has a match, else no; the no is optional

Table 15. Miscellaneous constructs

Expression Syntax	Meaning
(?imnsx-imnsx)	Set or disable options in midpattern
(?#)	Inline comment
# [to end of line]	X-mode comment

Table 16. Regular-expression options

Option	Meaning
i	Case-insensitive match
m	Multiline mode; changes ^ and $ so they match beginning and end of any line
n	Capture explicitly named or numbered groups
s	Single-line mode; changes meaning of "." so it matches every character
x	Eliminates unescaped whitespace from the pattern

Format Specifiers

Table 17 lists the numericformat specifiers supported by the Format method on the predefined numeric types.

Table 17. Numeric format specifiers

Specifier	String result	Datatype
C[n]	\$XX,XX.XX ($XX,XXX.XX)	Currency
D[n]	[-]XXXXXXX	Decimal
E[n] or e[n]	[-]X.XXXXXXE+xxx [-]X.XXXXXXe+xxx [-]X.XXXXXXE-xxx [-]X.XXXXXXe-xxx	Exponent
F[n]	[-]XXXXXXX.XX	Fixed point
G[n]	General or scientific	General
N[n]	[-]XX,XXX.XX	Number
X[n] or x[n]	Hex representation	Hex

This example uses a variety of numeric format specifiers:

```
using System;
class TestDefaultFormats {
  static void Main() {
```

```
// no precision specifiers
int i = 654321;
Console.WriteLine("{0:C}", i); // $654,321.00
Console.WriteLine("{0:D}", i); // 654321
Console.WriteLine("{0:E}", i); // 6.543210E+005
Console.WriteLine("{0:F}", i); // 654321.00
Console.WriteLine("{0:G}", i); // 654321
Console.WriteLine("{0:N}", i); // 654,321.00
Console.WriteLine("{0:X}", i); // 9FBF1
Console.WriteLine("{0:x}", i); // 9fbf1

// use precision specifiers
i = 123;
Console.WriteLine("{0:C6}", i); // $123.000000
Console.WriteLine("{0:D6}", i); // 000123
Console.WriteLine("{0:E6}", i); // 1.230000E+002
Console.WriteLine("{0:G6}", i); // 123
Console.WriteLine("{0:N6}", i); // 123.000000
Console.WriteLine("{0:X6}", i); // 00007B

// use a double value
double d = 1.23;
Console.WriteLine("{0:C6}", d); // $1.230000
Console.WriteLine("{0:E6}", d); // 1.230000E+000
Console.WriteLine("{0:G6}", d); // 1.23
Console.WriteLine("{0:N6}", d); // 1.230000
    }
}
```

Picture Format Specifiers

Table 18 lists the valid picture format specifiers supported by
the Format method on the predefined numeric types (see
System.IFormattable in the .NET Framework SDK
Documentation).

Table 18. Picture-format specifiers

Specifier	String result
0	Zero placeholder
#	Digit placeholder
.	Decimal point
,	Group separator or multiplier

Table 18. Picture-format specifiers (continued)

Specifier	String result
%	Percent notation
E0, E+0, E-0, e0, e+0, e-0	Exponent notation
\	Literal character quote
'xx', "xx"	Literal string quote
;	Section separator

This example uses picture-format specifiers on various values:

```
using System;
class TestIntegerCustomFormats {
  static void Main() {
    int i = 123;
    Console.WriteLine("{0:#0}", i);              // 123
    Console.WriteLine("{0:#0;(#0)}", i);         // 123
    Console.WriteLine("{0:#0;(#0);<zero>}", i);  // 123
    Console.WriteLine("{0:#%}", i);              // 12300%

    double d = 1.23;
    Console.WriteLine("{0:#.000E+00}", d);       // 1.230E+00
    Console.WriteLine(
      "{0:#.000E+00;(#.000E+00)}", d);           // 1.230E+00
    Console.WriteLine(
      "{0:#.000E+00;(#.000E+00);<zero>}", d);    // 1.230E+00
    Console.WriteLine("{0:#%}", d);              // 123%
  }
}
```

DateTime Format Specifiers

Table 19 lists the valid format specifiers supported by the Format method on the DateTime type (see the "Date and Time Format Strings" topic in the .NET Framework SDK Documentation).

Table 19. DateTime format specifiers

Specifier	String result
d	MM/dd/yyyy
D	dddd, MMMM dd, yyyy

Table 19. DateTime format specifiers (continued)

Specifier	String result
f	dddd, MMMM dd, yyyy HH:mm
F	dddd, MMMM dd, yyyy HH:mm:ss
g	MM/dd/yyyy HH:mm
G	MM/dd/yyyy HH:mm:ss
m, M	MMMM dd
r, R	Ddd, dd MMM yyyy HH':'mm':'ss 'GMT'
s	yyyy-MM-dd HH:mm:ss
S	yyyy-MM-dd HH:mm:ss GMT
t	HH:mm
T	HH:mm:ss
u	yyyy-MM-dd HH:mm:ss
U	dddd, MMMM dd, yyyy HH:mm:ss
y, Y	MMMM, yyyy

Here's an example that uses these custom format specifiers on a DateTime value:

```
using System;
class TestDateTimeFormats {
  static void Main() {
    DateTime dt = new DateTime(2000, 10, 11, 15, 32, 14);
    // Prints "10/11/2000 3:32:14 PM"
    Console.WriteLine(dt.ToString());
    // Prints "10/11/2000 3:32:14 PM"
    Console.WriteLine("{0}", dt);
    // Prints "10/11/2000"
    Console.WriteLine("{0:d}", dt);
    // Prints "Wednesday, October 11, 2000"
    Console.WriteLine("{0:D}", dt);
    // Prints "Wednesday, October 11, 2000 3:32 PM"
    Console.WriteLine("{0:f}", dt);
    // Prints "Wednesday, October 11, 2000 3:32:14 PM"
    Console.WriteLine("{0:F}", dt);
    // Prints "10/11/2000 3:32 PM"
    Console.WriteLine("{0:g}", dt);
```

```
      // Prints "10/11/2000 3:32:14 PM"
      Console.WriteLine("{0:G}", dt);
      // Prints "October 11"
      Console.WriteLine("{0:m}", dt);
      // Prints "October 11"
      Console.WriteLine("{0:M}", dt);
      // Prints "Wed, 11 Oct 2000 22:32:14 GMT"
      Console.WriteLine("{0:r}", dt);
      // Prints "Wed, 11 Oct 2000 22:32:14 GMT"
      Console.WriteLine("{0:R}", dt);
      // Prints "3:32 PM"
      Console.WriteLine("{0:t}", dt);
      // Prints "3:32:14 PM"
      Console.WriteLine("{0:T}", dt);
      // Prints "2000-10-11 15:32:14Z"
      Console.WriteLine("{0:u}", dt);
      // Prints "Wednesday, October 11, 2000 10:32:14 PM"
      Console.WriteLine("{0:U}", dt);
      // Prints "October, 2000"
      Console.WriteLine("{0:y}", dt);
      // Prints "October, 2000"
      Console.WriteLine("{0:Y}", dt);
      // Prints "Wednesday the 11 day of October in the year
      // 2000"
      Console.WriteLine(
        "{0:dddd 'the' d 'day of' MMMM 'in the year' yyyy}",
        dt);
  }
}
```

C# Compiler Options

The C# compiler, *csc.exe*, compiles C# sources and incorporates resource files and separately compiled modules. It also allows you to specify conditional compilation options, XML documentation, and path information.

Synopsis

```
csc [options] files
```

Examples

```
csc foo.cs /r:bar.dll /win32res:foo.res
csc foo.cs /debug /define:TEMP
```

Options

/?, /help
> Displays usage information and exits.

@*file*
> Specifies a response file containing arguments to *csc.exe*.

/addmodule:*file1*[;*file2* ...]
> Imports metadata from one or more named modules (files with the extension *.netmodule*). To create a module, use /target: module.

/baseaddress:*addr*
> Specifies the base address at which to load DLLs.

/bugreport:*file*
> Generates a text file that contains a bug report. Use this to report a bug in *csc.exe*.

/checked[+|-]
> If you specify /checked+, causes the runtime to throw an exception when an integer operation results in a value outside the range of the associated datatype. This only affects code that has not been wrapped in a checked or unchecked block of code. If you specify /checked-, an exception is not thrown.

/codepage:*id*
> Specifies the code page to use for all source files.

/d[efine]:*symbol1*[;*symbol2* ...]
> Specify one or more symbols to define. This has the same effect as the #define preprocessor directive.

/debug[+|-]
> Enables or disables debugging information. You may specify /debug instead of /debug+. The default is /debug-.

/debug:(full|pdbonly)
> Specifies the debug modes that are supported by the generated assembly. The full option is the default and allows you to perform source-code debugging when attaching a debugger to the program before or after it is started. The pdbonly option only permits source-code debugging if you start the program under control of the debugger. If you attach the debugger to the program after it is started, it displays only native assembly in the debugger.

/doc:*file*

    Specifies the XML documentation file to generate.

/filealign:*size*

    Specifies the size, in bytes, of sections in the output file. Valid sizes are 512, 1024, 2048, 4096, 8192, and 16384.

/fullpaths

    Use fully qualified filenames in error messages.

/incr[emental][+|-]

    Enables or disables incremental compilation. By default, incremental compilation is off.

/lib:*dir1*[;*dir2* ...]

    Specifies directories to search for assemblies imported with the /reference option.

/linkres[ource]:*file*[,*id*]

    Specifies a .NET resource (and optional identifier) to link to the generated assembly. Not valid with /target:module.

/m[ain]:*type*

    Specifies the name of the type that contains the entry point. This is only valid for executables. The entry point method must be named Main and must be declared static.

/noconfig

    Specifies not to use the global or local configuration file (*csc.rsp*). You can find the global *csc.rsp* file in *%SystemRoot%\Microsoft.NET\Framework\VERSION*, in which *VERSION* is a version of the .NET Framework. This file contains default arguments for the C# compiler, including the list of assemblies that are imported by default. If you create a file named *csc.rsp* in the same directory as your source code, it is processed after the global configuration file.

/nologo

    Suppresses display of the banner and copyright messages.

/nostdlib[+|-]

    With /nostdlib+ or /nostdlib, causes the C# compiler to import *mscorlib.dll*, which defines the fundamental types used in .NET and most of the System namespace.

/nowarn:*number1*[;*number2* ...]

    Specifies a list of warning numbers to ignore. Do not include the alphabetic part of the warning. For example, to suppress warning *CS0169*, use /nowarn:169.

/o[ptimize][+|-]

    Enables or disables compiler optimizations. By default, optimizations are enabled.

/out:*file*

    Specifies the output filename.

/recurse:*wildcard*

    Recursively searches directories for source-code files matching *wildcard* (which may include directory names).

/r[eference]:*file1*[;*file2* ...]

    Imports metadata from one or more named assemblies. Generally used with DLLs, but you may also specify executables.

/res[ource]:*file*[,*id*]

    Specifies a .NET resource (and optional identifier) to embed in the generated assembly.

/t[arget]:*format*

    Specifies the format of the output file. The valid formats are library (DLL library), module (a library without an assembly manifest), exe (console application), or winexe (Windows application).

/unsafe[+|-]

    Enables or disables (the default) unsafe code. Unsafe code is enclosed in a block marked by the unsafe keyword.

/utf8output

    Displays compiler console output using UTF-8 encoding.

/w[arn]:*level*

    Sets the compiler warning level from 0 (no warnings) to 4 (the default, all warnings).

/warnaserror[+|-]

    Enables or disables (the default) treating warnings as errors (warnings halt compilation).

/win32icon:file
> Specifies an icon (*.ico*) file to use as the application's icon.

/win32res:file
> Specifies a Win32 resource (*.res*) file to insert in the output file.

Essential .NET Tools

The .NET Framework SDK contains many useful programming tools. Here, in an alphabetical list, are those we have found most useful or necessary for developing C# applications. Unless otherwise noted, the tools in this list can be found either in the *\bin* directory of your .NET Framework SDK installation or in the *%SystemRoot%\Microsoft.NET\Framework\VERSION* directory (replace *VERSION* with the framework version). Once the .NET Framework is installed, you can access these tools from any directory. To use any of these tools, invoke a Command Prompt window, and enter the name of the desired tool. For a complete list of the available command-line switches for any given tool, enter the tool name (e.g., csc), and press the Return key.

ADepends.exe: assembly dependency list
> Displays all assemblies on which a given assembly is dependent to load. This is a useful C# program found among the samples in the *\Tool Developers Guide* directory beneath the .NET Framework or Visual Studio .NET directory tree. You need to install these samples before you can use them, because they are not installed by default.

Al.exe: assembly linking utility
> Creates an assembly manifest from the modules and resources files you name. You can also include Win32 resources files. Here's an example:
>
> ```
> al /out:c.dll a.netmodule b.netmodule
> ```

CorDbg.exe: runtime debugger

General source-level, command-line debug utility for MSIL programs. This is a very useful tool for C# source debugging. The source for *cordbg* is available in the *\Tool Developers Guide* directory.

Csc.exe: C# compiler

Compiles C# sources and incorporates resource files and separately compiled modules; also allows you to specify conditional compilation options, XML documentation, and path information. Here are some examples:

```
csc foo.cs /r:bar.dll /win32res:foo.res
csc foo.cs /debug /define:TEMP
```

DbgClr.exe: GUI debugger

Windows-based, source-level debugger. This is available in the *\GuiDebug* directory of the .NET Framework SDK installation.

GACUtil.exe: global assembly cache utility

Allows you to install, uninstall, and list the contents of the global assembly cache. Here's an example:

```
gacutil /i c.dll
```

ILAsm.exe: MSIL assembler

Creates MSIL modules and assemblies directly from an MSIL textual representation.

ILDasm.exe: MSIL disassembler

Disassembles modules and assemblies. The default is to display a tree-style representation, but you can also specify an output file. Here are some examples:

```
ildasm b.dll
ildasm b.dll /out=b.asm
```

InstallUtil.exe: installer utility

Executes installers and uninstallers contained within the assembly. A log file can be written, and state information can be persisted.

Ngen.exe: native image generator

Compiles an assembly to native code and installs a native image in the local assembly cache. That native image is used each time you access the original assembly, even though the original assembly contains MSIL. If the runtime can't locate the native image, it falls back on JIT compilation. Here are some examples:

```
ngen foo.exe
ngen foo.dll
```

nmake.exe: make utility

Common utility that scripts building of multiple components and source files and tracks rebuild dependency information.

PEVerify.exe: portable executable verifier

Verifies that your compiler has generated type-safe MSIL. C# will always generate type-safe MSIL. It has useful interop with ILASM-based programs.

RegAsm.exe: register assembly tool

Registers an assembly in the system registry. This allows COM clients to call managed methods. You can also use it to generate the registry file for future registration. Here's an example:

```
regasm /regfile:c.reg c.dll
```

RegSvcs.exe: register services utility

Registers an assembly to COM+ 1.0 and installs its typelib into an existing application. This can also generate a typelib. Here's an example:

```
regsvcs foo.dll /appname:comapp /tlb:newfoo.tlb
```

Sn.exe: shared name utility

Verifies assemblies and their key information; also generates key files. Here's an example:

```
sn -k mykey.snk
```

SoapSuds.exe: SoapSuds utility

Creates XML schemas for services in an assembly and creates assemblies from a schema. You can also reference the schema via its URL. Here's an example:

```
soapsuds
    -url:http://localhost/myapp/app.soap?wsdl
    -os:app.xml
```

TlbExp.exe: type library exporter

Exports a COM typelib derived from the public types within the supplied assembly. Differs from *regasm* in that it doesn't perform any registration. Here's an example:

```
tlbexp /out:c.tlb c.dll
```

TlbImp.exe: type library importer

Creates a managed assembly from the supplied COM typelib, mapping the type definitions to .NET types. You need to import this new assembly into your C# program for use. Here's an example:

```
tlbimp /out:MyOldCom.dll MyCom.tlb
```

Wsdl.exe: web services description language tool

Creates service descriptions and generates proxies for ASP.NET web-service methods. See the ASP.NET documentation in the .NET Framework SDK Documentation for more detail on web services.

WinCV.exe: windows class viewer

Searches for matching names within a supplied assembly. If none are supplied, it uses the default libraries. The namespaces and classes are displayed in a listbox, and the selected type information is displayed in another window.

Xsd.exe: XML schema definition tool

Generates XML schemas from XDR, XML files, or class information. Can also generate DataSet or class information from a schema. Here's an example:

```
xsd foo.xdr
xsd bar.dll
```

Index

We'd like to hear your suggestions for improving our indexes. Send email to
index@oreilly.com.